Mexican Spanish
Phrase Book
&
Dictionary

Berlitz Publishing
New York Munich Singapore

Contacting the Editors
Every effort has been made to provide accurate information in this publication, but changes are inevitable. The publisher cannot be responsible for any resulting loss, inconvenience or injury. We would appreciate it if readers would call our attention to any errors or outdated information. We also welcome your suggestions; if you come across a relevant expression not in our phrase book, please contact us: Berlitz Publishing, 193 Morris Avenue, Springfield, NJ 07081, USA. E-mail: comments@berlitzbooks.com

Second Printing: October 2009
Printed in Singapore

Publishing Director: Sheryl Olinsky Borg
Senior Editor/Project Manager: Lorraine Sova
Cover Design: Claudia Petrilli
Interior Design: Derrick Lim, Juergen Bartz
Production Manager: Elizabeth Gaynor
Localization & Composition: D&M Language Services
Cover Photo: © John DiGiorgio
Interior Photos: p. 12 © Studio Fourteen/Brand X Pictures/age fotostock; p. 16 © Emin Kuliyev, 2006. Used under license from Shutterstock, Inc.; p. 18 © 2008 Jupiterimages Corporation; p. 21 © Pixtal/age fotostock; p. 37 © D&M Language Services; p. 40 © Corbis/fotosearch.com; p.52 © Purestock/Alamy; p. 58 © David Smith - Fotolia.com; p. 61 © Stockbyte Photography/2002-07 Veer Incorporated; p. 73 © Quendi Language Services; p. 87 © Javier Larrea/Pixtal/age fotostock; p.88 © Gustavo Acosta/Alamy; p. 90 © Netfalls/2003-2007 Shutterstock, Inc.; p. 107 © Blend Images/Alamy; p. 109 © Mel Wineburger/Alamy; p. 115 © image100/Corbis; p. 118 © Jupiterimages/Brand X/Alamy; p. 121 © Steve Hamblin/Alamy; p. 124 © 2007 Jupiterimages Corporation; p. 132 © deserttrends - Fotolia.com; p. 141 © 2007 Jupiterimages Corporation; p. 150 © Blend Images/Alamy; p. 151 © Jupiterimages/Brand X/Corbis; p. 153 © Stockbyte/Fotosearch.com; p. 156 © Corbis/2006 Jupiterimages Corporation; p. 159 © David McKee/2003-2007 Shutterstock, Inc.; p. 160, 169, 180 © 2007 Jupiterimages Corporation; p. 166 © Corbis/age fotostock

Contents

Survival

Food

People

Fun

Special Needs

Resources

Dictionary

Pronunciation

This section is designed to make you familiar with the sounds of Mexican Spanish using our simplified phonetic transcription. You'll find the pronunciation of the Spanish letters and sounds explained below, together with their "imitated" equivalents. This system is used throughout the phrase book; simply read the pronunciation as if it were English, noting any special rules below.

Underlined letters indicate that that syllable should be stressed. The acute accent ´ indicates stress, e.g. **río**, <u>rree</u>•oh. Some Spanish words have more than one meaning. In these instances, the accent mark is also used to distinguish between them, e.g.: **él** (he) and **el** (the); **sí** (yes) and **si** (if).

There are some differences in vocabulary and pronunciation between the Spanish spoken in Spain and that in the Americas—although each is easily understood by the other. This phrase book and dictionary is specifically geared to travelers in Mexico.

Consonants

Letter	Approximate Pronunciation	Symbol	Example	Pronunciation
b	1. as in English	b	**bueno**	<u>bweh</u>•noh
	2. between vowels as in English, but softer	b	**bebida**	beh•<u>bee</u>•dah
c	1. before e and i like s in same	s	**centro**	<u>sehn</u>•troh
	2. otherwise like k in kit	k	**como**	<u>koh</u>•moh
ch	as in English	ch	**mucho**	<u>moo</u>•choh
g	1. before e and i, like ch in Scottish loch	kh	**urgente**	oor•<u>khehn</u>•teh
	2. otherwise, like g in get	g	**ninguno**	neen•<u>goo</u>•noh

Letter	Approximate Pronunciation	Symbol	Example	Pronunciation
h	always silent		**hombre**	ohm•breh
j	like ch in Scottish loch	kh	**bajo**	bah•khoh
ll	like y in yellow	y	**lleno**	yeh•noh
ñ	like ni in onion	ny	**señor**	seh•nyohr
q	like k in kick	k	**quince**	keen•seh
r	1. at the beginning of a word or after n, l or s, strongly trilled	rr	**río**	rree•oh
	2. otherwise, softly trilled	r	**marzo**	mahr•soh
rr	strongly trilled	rr	**arriba**	ah•rree•bah
s	1. like s in same	s	**sus**	soos
	2. before b, d, g, l, m, n, like s in rose	z	**mismo**	meez•moh
v	like b in bad, but softer	b	**viejo**	beeyeh•khoh
x	1. at the beginning of a word, like s in same or like ch in Scottish loch	s, kh	**Xochimilco, xilófono**	soh•chee•meel•koh khee•loh•foh•noh
	2. in some words of Aztec origin, like ch in Scottish loch	kh	**México**	meh•khee•coh
	3. otherwise as in English	x	**exámen**	eh•xah•mehn
z	like s in same	s	**brazo**	brah•soh

Letters d, f, k, l, m, n, p, t, w and y are pronounced as in English.

Vowels

Letter	Approximate Pronunciation	Symbol	Example	Pronunciation
a	like the a in father	ah	**gracias**	grah·seeyahs
e	like e in get	eh	**esta**	ehs·tah
i	like ee in meet	ee	**sí**	see
o	like o in rope	oh	**dos**	dohs
u	1. like oo in food	oo	**uno**	oo·noh
	2. silent after g and q		**que**	keh
	3. when marked ü, like w in well	w	**agüero**	ah·gweh·roh
y	1. like y in yellow	y	**hoy**	oy
	2. when alone, like ee in meet	ee	**y**	ee
	3. when preceded by an a, sounds like y + ee, with ee faintly pronounced	aye	**hay**	aye

The **Estados Unidos Mexicanos** (United Mexican States) or simply **México** (Mexico), is a federal constitutional republic in North America. Mexico is a federation comprising thirty-one states and a federal district. The capital, Mexico City, is one of the world's most populous cities.

Although there is no official language at the federal level in Mexico, Spanish is spoken by 97% of the population.

Mexican Spanish is also widely spoken by immigrant communities in the United States.

How to Use This Book

These essential phrases can also be heard on the audio CD.

Sometimes you see two alternatives in italics, separated by a slash. Choose the one that's right for your situation.

Essential

I'm on *vacation [holiday]/business.*	**Estoy aquí *de vacaciones/en viaje de negocios.*** ehs·toy ah·kee *deh bah·kah·seeyoh·nehs/ehn beeyah·kheh deh neh·goh·seeyohs*
I'm going to...	**Voy a...** boy ah...
I'm staying at the... Hotel.	**Me alojo en el Hotel...** meh ah·loh·khoh ehn ehl oh·tehl...

You May See...

ADUANAS	customs
ARTÍCULOS LIBRES DE IMPUESTOS	duty-free goods
ARTÍCULOS QUE DECLARAR	goods to declare

Bicycle and Motorcycle

I'd like to rent [hire]...	**Quiero rentar...** keeyeh·roh rrehn·tahr...
– a bicycle	**– una bicicleta** oo·nah bee·see·kleh·tah
– a moped	**– una motoneta** oo·nah moh·toh·neh·tah
– a motorcycle	**– una motocicleta** oo·nah moh·toh·see·kleh·tah
How much per *day/week*?	**¿Cuánto cuesta por *día/semana*?** kwahn·toh kwehs·tah pohr *dee·ah/seh·mah·nah*

Words you may see are shown in *You May See* boxes.

Any of the words or phrases preceded by dashes can be plugged into the sentence above.

Spanish phrases appear in red.

Read the simplified pronunciation as if it were English. For more on pronunciation, see page 7.

Pick-up [Chat-up] Lines

Can I join you? **¿Puedo acompañarlo♂/acompañarla♀?**
pweh•doh ah•kohm•pah•nyahr•loh♂/ ah•kohm•pah•nyahr•la[illegible]

You're very attractive. **Es muy guapo♂/g[illegible]**
ehs mooy gwah•poh♂[illegible]

Let's go somewhere quieter. **Vayamos a un siti[illegible]**
bah•yah•mohs ah oon see•teeyoh mahs trahn•kee•loh

When different gender forms apply, the masculine form is followed by ♂; feminine by ♀.

▶For informal and formal "you", see page 172.

The arrow indicates a cross reference where you'll find related phrases.

Information boxes contain relevant country, culture and language tips.

In Spanish, there are a number of forms for "you", taking different verb forms: **tú** (singular, informal), **usted** (singular, formal) and **ustedes** (plural). When addressing strangers, always use the more formal **usted** (singular) as opposed to the more familiar **tú** (singular), until told otherwise.

You May Hear...

Hablo muy poco inglés. I only speak a little English.
ah•bloh mooy poh•koh een•glehs

Expressions you may hear are shown in *You May Hear* boxes.

Color-coded side bars identify each section of the book.

▼ Survival

Arrival and Departure

Essential

I'm on *vacation [holiday]/business.* **Estoy aquí *de vacaciones/en viaje de negocios.*** ehs·toy ah·kee *deh bah·kah·seeyoh·nehs/ehn beeyah·kheh deh neh·goh·seeyohs*

I'm going to... **Voy a...** boy ah...

I'm staying at the... Hotel. **Me alojo en el Hotel...** meh ah·loh·khoh ehn ehl oh·tehl...

You May Hear...

Su pasaporte, por favor. soo pah·sah·pohr·teh pohr fah·bohr
Your passport, please.

¿Cuál es el propósito de su visita? kwahl ehs ehl proh·poh·see·toh deh soo bee·see·tah
What's the purpose of your visit?

¿Dónde se aloja? dohn·deh seh ah·loh·khah
Where are you staying?

¿Cuánto tiempo piensa quedarse? kwahn·toh teeyehm·poh peeyehn·sah keh·dar·seh
How long are you staying?

¿Con quién viaja? kohn keeyehn beeyah·khah
Who are you here with?

Passport Control and Customs

I'm just passing through. **Estoy de paso.** ehs·toy deh pah·soh

I'd like to declare... **Quiero declarar...** keeyeh·roh deh·klah·rahr...

I have nothing to declare. **No tengo nada que declarar.** noh tehn·goh nah·dah keh deh·klah·rahr

You May Hear…

¿Tiene algo que declarar?
teeyeh•neh ahl•goh keh deh•klah•rahr
Anything to declare?

Tiene que pagar impuestos por esto.
teeyeh•neh keh pah•gahr eem•pwehs•tohs pohr ehs•toh
You must pay duty on this.

Abra esta maleta.
ah•brah ehs•tah mah•leh•tah
Open this bag.

You May See…

ADUANA	customs
ARTÍCULOS LIBRES DE IMPUESTOS	duty-free goods
ARTÍCULOS QUE DECLARAR	goods to declare
NADA QUE DECLARAR	nothing to declare
CONTROL DE PASAPORTES	passport control
POLICÍA	police

In order to pass the Mexican border, you must submit a completed Customs Declaration Form. Items destined for personal use do not need to be declared. However, the values of extra items that you bring in the country do. Limits vary depending on whether you enter the country by air, sea or land. Incorrectly reporting the value of an item or not declaring an item may be penalized by fines and/or possible confiscation.

Money and Banking

Essential

Where's...?	**¿Dónde está...?** dohn·deh ehs·tah...
– the ATM	**– el cajero automático** ehl kah·kheh·roh aw·toh·mah·tee·koh
– the bank	**– el banco** ehl bahn·koh
– the currency exchange office	**– la casa de cambio** lah kah·sah deh kahm·beeyoh
When does the bank *open/close*?	**¿A qué hora *abre/cierra* el banco?** ah keh oh·rah *ah·breh/seeyeh·rrah* ehl bahn·koh
I'd like to change *dollars/pounds* into pesos.	**Quiero cambiar *dólares/libras* a pesos.** keeyeh·roh kahm·beeyahr *doh·lah·rehs/lee·brahs* ah peh·sohs
I'd like to cash traveler's checks [cheques].	**Quiero cobrar cheques de viajero.** keeyeh·roh koh·brahr cheh·kehs deh beeyah·kheh·roh

▶For currency, see page 18.

ATM, Bank and Currency Exchange

I'd like to change money.	**Quiero cambiar dinero.** keeyeh·roh kahm·beeyahr dee·neh·roh
What's the exchange rate?	**¿Cuál es el tipo de cambio?** kwahl ehs ehl tee·poh deh kahm·beeyoh
How much is the fee?	**¿Cuánto es la comisión?** kwahn·toh ehs lah·koh mee see·yohn
I lost my traveler's checks [cheques].	**Perdí mis cheques de viajero.** pehr·dee mees cheh·kehs deh beeyah·kheh·roh

My card was lost.	**Perdí mí tarjeta.** pehr·dee mee tahr·kheh·tah
My card was stolen.	**Me robaron la tarjeta.** meh rroh·bah·rohn lah tahr·kheh·tah
My card doesn't work.	**Mi tarjeta no funciona.** mee tahr·kheh·tah noh foon·seeyoh·nah

►For numbers, see page 178.

You May See...

INTRODUCIR TARJETA AQUÍ	insert card here
CANCELAR	cancel
BORRAR	clear
INTRODUCIR	enter
NIP	PIN
RETIRAR FONDOS	withdraw funds
DE CUENTA DE CHEQUES	from checking [current account]
DE CUENTA DE AHORROS	from savings
COMPROBANTE	receipt

i

ATMs are located throughout major cities in Mexico and are networked to the Cirrus, PLUS and several other systems. Cash can be obtained from ATMs with Visa™, MasterCard™ and many other cards. Be aware that Mexican ATMs charge fees for balance inquiries, cash withdrawals and other operations. Instructions are given in Spanish, but many ATMs located at international airports and major tourist destinations have instructions in English and may even dispense U.S. dollars. Debit cards are becoming a more accepted method of payment in Mexico, but to be sure ask if they are accepted (for example, convenience stores may only accept cash). Whether using a credit card or debit card, make sure you have your PIN (personal identification number) and that it is four digits. If you have an alphabetic PIN, be aware that Mexican ATMs don't have letters on the keypad.

The best rates for exchanging money will be found at banks. You can change money at currency exchange agencies, travel agencies and hotels, but the rate will not be as good. Remember your passport when you want to change money.

Mexican currency is the **peso** ($), divided into 100 **centavos** (cents).

Monedas (coins): 10, 20, 50 **centavos**, 1, 2, 5, 10 **pesos**.
Billetes (notes): 20, 50, 100, 200, 500, 1000 **pesos**.

Note: Most businesses do not accept the $1,000 note, but it can be exchanged at banks.

Transportation

Essential

How do I get to town?	**¿Cómo se llega a la ciudad?** koh·moh seh yeh·gah ah lah seew·dahd
Where's...?	**¿Dónde está...?** dohn·deh ehs·tah...
– the airport	**– el aeropuerto** ehl ah·eh·roh·pwehr·toh
– the train [railway] station	**– la estación del tren** lah ehs·tah·seeyohn dehl trehn
– the bus station	**– la estación de camiones** lah ehs·tah·seeyohn deh kah·meeyoh·nehs
– the subway [underground] station	**– la estación del metro** lah ehs·tah·seeyohn dehl meh·troh
How far is it?	**¿A qué distancia está?** ah keh dees·tahn·seeyah ehs·tah
Where can I buy a ticket?	**¿Dónde puedo comprar el boleto?** dohn·deh pweh·doh kohm·prahr ehl boh·leh·toh
A *one-way/round-trip [return]* ticket to...	**Un boleto *sencillo/redondo* a...** oon boh·leh·toh *sehn·see·yoh/rreh·dohn·doh* ah...
How much?	**¿Cuánto es?** kwahn·toh ehs
Is there a discount?	**¿Hacen descuento?** ah·sen dehs·kwehn·toh
Which...?	**¿Cuál...?** kwahl...
– gate	**– puerta de embarque** pwehr·tah deh ehm·bahr·keh
– line	**– línea** lee·neh·ah
– platform	**– andén** ahn·dehn
Where can I get a taxi?	**¿Dónde puedo tomar un taxi?** dohn·deh pweh·doh toh·mahr oon tah·xee

Take me to this address.	**Lléveme a esta dirección.** yeh·beh·meh ah ehs·tah dee·rehk·seeyohn
Where's the car rental [hire]?	**¿Dónde está la renta de autos?** dohn·deh ehs·tah lah rrehn·tah deh aw·tohs
Can I have a map?	**¿Puede darme un mapa?** pweh·deh dahr·meh oon mah·pah

Ticketing

When's...to Acapulco?	**¿Cuándo sale...a Acapulco?** kwahn·doh sah·leh...ah ah·kah·pool·koh
– the (first) bus	**– el (primer) camión** ehl (pree·mehr) kah·meeyohn
– the (next) flight	**– el (siguiente) vuelo** ehl (see·geeyehn·teh) bweh·loh
– the (last) train	**– el (último) tren** ehl (ool·tee·moh) trehn
Where do I buy a ticket?	**¿Dónde puedo comprar el boleto?** dohn·deh pweh·doh kohm·prahr ehl boh·leh·toh
One/Two ticket(s), please.	***Un/Dos* boleto(s), por favor.** *oon/dohs* boh·leh·toh(s) pohr fah·bohr
For *today/tomorrow*.	**Para *hoy/mañana*.** pah·rah *oy/mah·nyah·nah*
...ticket.	**Un boleto...** oon boh·leh·toh...
– A one-way	**– sencillo** sehn·see·yoh
– A round-trip [return]	**– redondo** rreh·dohn·doh
– A first-class	**– de primera clase** deh pree·meh·rah klah·seh
– An economy-class	**– de clase turista** deh klah·seh tuh·rees·tah

▶For time, see page 180.

▶For days, see page 181.

How much?	**¿Cuánto es?** kwahn•toh ehs
Is there a... discount?	**¿Hacen descuento a...?** ah•sehn dehs•kwehn•toh ah...
– child	**– niños** nee•nyohs
– student	**– estudiantes** ehs•too•deeyahn•tehs
– senior citizen	**– personas de la tercera edad** pehr•soh•nahs deh lah tehr•seh•rah eh•dahd
Can I buy a ticket on the *bus/train*?	**¿Puedo comprar el boleto a bordo del *camión/tren*?** pweh•doh kohm•prahr ehl boh•leh•toh ah bohr•doh dehl *kah•meeyohn/trehn*
I'd like to...my reservation.	**Quiero...mi reserva.** keeyeh•roh...mee rreh•sehr•bah
– cancel	**– cancelar** kahn•seh•lahr
– change	**– cambiar** kahm•beeyahr
– confirm	**– confirmar** kohn•feer•mahr

Plane

Getting to the Airport

How much is a taxi to the airport?	**¿Cuánto es la dejada al aeropuerto?** kwahn·toh ehs lah deh·jah·dah ahl ah·eh·roh·pwehr·toh
To...Airport, please.	**Al aeropuerto de..., por favor.** ahl ah·eh·roh·pwehr·toh deh...pohr fah·bohr
My airline is...	**Mi aerolínea es...** mee ah·eh·roh·lee·neh·ah ehs...
My flight leaves at...	**Mi vuelo sale a la/las...** mee bweh·loh sah·leh ah lah/lahs...

▶For when to use **la** or **las**, see page 174.

▶For time, see page 180.

I'm in a rush.	**Tengo prisa.** tehn·goh pree·sah
Can you take an alternate route?	**¿Puede tomar otra ruta?** pweh·deh toh·mahr oh·trah rroo·tah
Can you drive *faster/slower*?	**¿Puede ir más *deprisa/despacio*?** pweh·deh eer mahs *deh·pree·sah/dehs·pah·seeyoh*

You May Hear...

¿En qué aerolínea viaja? ehn keh ah·eh·roh·lee·neh·ah beeyah·khah	What airline are you flying?
¿Nacional o internacional? nah·seeyoh·nahl oh een·tehr·nah·seeyoh·nahl	Domestic or international?
¿Qué terminal? keh tehr·mee·nahl	What terminal?

You May See...

LLEGADAS	arrivals
SALIDAS	departures

RECLAMO DE EQUIPAJE	baggage claim
VUELOS NACIONALES	domestic flights
VUELOS INTERNACIONALES	international flights
MOSTRADOR DE DOCUMENTACIÓN	check-in
DOCUMENTACIÓN CON BOLETO ELECTRÓNICO	e-ticket check-in
SALAS DE ABORDAR	departure gates

Check-in and Boarding

Where's check-in?	**¿Dónde está el mostrador de documentación?** dohn·deh ehs·tah ehl mohs·trah·dohr deh doh·koo·mehn·tah·seeyohn
My name is...	**Me llamo...** meh yah·moh...
I'm going to...	**Voy a...** boy ah...
How much luggage is allowed?	**¿Cuánto equipaje está permitido?** kwahn·toh eh·kee·pah·kheh ehs·tah pehr·mee·tee·doh
Which *terminal/gate*?	**¿Qué *terminal/sala de abordar*?** keh *tehr·mee·nahl/sah·lah deh ah·bohr·dahr*
I'd like *a window/an aisle* seat.	**Quiero un asiento en *ventana/pasillo*.** keeyeh·roh oon ah·seeyehn·toh ehn *behn·tah·nah/pah·see·yoh*
When do we *leave/arrive*?	**¿A qué hora *salimos/llegamos*?** ah keh oh·rah *sah·lee·mohs/yeh·gah·mohs*
Is the flight delayed?	**¿Tiene retraso el vuelo?** teeyeh·neh rreh·trah·soh ehl bweh·loh
How late?	**¿Cuánto retraso tiene?** kwahn·toh rreh·trah·soh teeyeh·neh

You May Hear...

¡Siguiente! see·geeyehn·teh	Next!
Su *pasaporte/boleto*, por favor. *soo pah·sah·pohr·teh/boh·leh·toh* pohr fah·bohr	Your *passport/ticket*, please.
¿Va a documentar el equipaje? bah ah doh·koo·mehn·tahr ehl eh·kee·pah·kheh	Are you checking any luggage?
Lleva sobreequipaje. yeh·bah soh·breh eh·kee·pah·kheh	You have excess luggage.
Eso es demasiado grande para equipaje de mano. eh·soh ehs deh·mah·seeyah·doh grahn·deh pah·rah eh·kee·pah·kheh deh mah·noh	That's too large for a carry-on [to carry on board].
¿Hizo usted las maletas? ee·soh oos·ted lahs mah·leh·tahs	Did you pack these bags yourself?
¿Le entregó alguien algún paquete? leh ehn·treh·goh ahl·geeyehn ahl·goon pah·keh·teh	Did anyone give you anything to carry?
Vacíese los bolsillos. bah·see·eh·seh lohs bohl·see·yohs	Empty your pockets.
Quítese los zapatos. kee·teh·seh lohs sah·pah·tohs	Take off your shoes.
El vuelo...está abordando. ehl bweh·loh...ehs·tah ah·bohr·dahn·doh	Now boarding flight...

Luggage

Where *is/are*...?	**¿Dónde *está/están*...?** dohn deh *ehs·tah/ehs·tahn*...
– the luggage carts [trolleys]	**– los carritos para equipaje** lohs kah·rree·tohs pah·rah eh·kee·pah·kheh

– the luggage lockers	**– los casilleros para equipaje** lohs kah•see•yeh•rohs pah•rah eh•kee•pah•kheh
– the baggage claim	**– el reclamo de equipaje** ehl rreh•klah•moh deh eh•kee•pah•kheh
My luggage has been lost.	**Mi equipaje está perdido.** mee eh•kee•pah•kheh ehs•tah pehr•dee•doh
My luggage has been stolen.	**Me robaron el equipaje.** meh rroh•bah•rohn ehl eh•kee•pah•kheh
My suitcase is damaged.	**Mi maleta está dañada.** mee mah•leh•tah ehs•tah dah•nyah•dah

Finding Your Way

Where *is/are*...?	**¿Dónde *está/están*...?** dohn•deh *ehs•tah/ehs•tahn*...
– the currency exchange	**– la casa de cambio** lah kah•sah deh kahm•beeyoh
– the car rental [hire]	**– la renta de autos** lah rrehn•tah deh aw•tohs
– the exit	**– la salida** lah sah•lee•dah
– the taxis	**– los taxis** lohs tah•xees
Is there...into town?	**¿Hay...que vaya a la ciudad?** aye...keh bah•yah ah lah seew•dahd
– a bus	**– un camión** oon kah•meeyohn
– a train	**– un tren** oon trehn
– a subway [underground]	**– un metro** oon meh•troh

▶For directions, see page 34.

Train

Where's the train [railway] station?	**¿Dónde está la estación del tren?** dohn·deh ehs·tah lah ehs·tah·seeyohn dehl trehn
How far is it?	**¿A qué distancia está?** ah keh dees·tahn·seeyah ehs·tah
Where *is/are*...?	**¿Dónde *está/están*...?** dohn·deh *ehs·tah/ehs·tahn*...
– the information desk	**– los módulos de información** lohs moh·doo·lohs deh een·fohr·mah·seeyohn
– the luggage lockers	**– los casilleros** lohs kah·see·yeh·rohs
– the platforms	**– los andenes** lohs ahn·deh·nehs
– the ticket office	**– la taquilla** lah tah·kee·yah

▶For directions, see page 34.

▶For ticketing, see page 20.

You May See...

ANDENES	platforms
INFORMACIÓN	information
RESERVAS	reservations
SALA DE ESPERA	waiting room
LLEGADAS	arrivals
SALIDAS	departures

Questions

Can I have a schedule [timetable]?	**¿Podría darme un itinerario?** poh·dree·ah dahr·meh oon ee·tee·neh·rah·reeyoh
How long is the trip?	**¿Cuánto dura el viaje?** kwahn·toh doo·rah ehl beeyah·kheh

Do I have to change trains?	**¿Tengo que transbordar?** tehn·goh keh trahnz·bohr·darh

Mexico has very limited passenger rail service. Instead, a plethora of private intercity bus lines serve this nation. The Chihuahua Pacific Express ("Chepe") is a notable exception, an engineering feat and a 630 km spectacular trip.

Departures

Which track [platform] for the train to...?	**¿De qué andén sale el tren a...?** deh keh ahn·dehn sah·leh ehl trehn ah...
Is this the *track [platform]/train* to...?	**¿Es éste el *andén/tren* a...?** ehs ehs·teh ehl *ahn·dehn/trehn* ah...
Where is track [platform]...?	**¿Dónde está el andén...?** dohn·deh ehs·tah ehl ahn·dehn...
Where do I change for...?	**¿Dónde tengo que transbordar para...?** dohn·deh tehn·goh keh trahnz·bohr·dahr pah·rah...

Boarding

Can I sit here?	**¿Puedo sentarme aquí?** pweh·doh sehn·tahr·meh ah·kee
That's my seat.	**Ése es mi asiento.** eh·seh ehs mee ah·seeyehn·toh

You May Hear...

¡Todos a bordo! toh·dohs ah bohr·doh	All aboard!
Boletos, por favor. boh·leh·tohs pohr fah·bohr	Tickets, please.
Tiene que transbordar en... teeyeh·neh keh trahnz·bohr·dahr ehn...	You have to change trains at...
Próxima parada: Chihuahua. proh·xee·mah pah·rah·dah chee·wah·wah	Next stop, Chihuahua.

Bus

Where's the bus station?	**¿Dónde está la estación de camiones?** dohn·deh ehs·tah lah ehs·tah·seeyohn deh kah·meeyoh·nehs
How far is it?	**¿A qué distancia está?** ah keh dees·tahn·seeyah ehs·tah
How do I get to…?	**¿Cómo llego a…?** koh·moh yeh·goh ah…
Is this the bus to…?	**¿Es éste el camión a…?** ehs ehs·teh ehl kah·meeyohn ah…
What's the fare to…?	**¿Cuál es la tarifa a…?** kwahl ehs lah tah·ree·fah ah…
Can you tell me when to get off?	**¿Podría decirme cuándo me tengo que bajar?** poh·dree·ah deh·seer·meh kwahn·doh meh tehn·goh keh bah·khahr
Do I have to change buses?	**¿Tengo que transbordar?** tehn·goh keh trahnz·bohr·dahr
How many stops to…?	**¿Cuántas paradas hay hasta…?** kwahn·tahs pah·rah·dahs aye ahs·tah…
Stop here, please!	**¡Pare aquí, por favor!** pah·reh ah·kee pohr fah·bohr

▶For ticketing, see page 20.

You May See…

PARADA DE CAMIONES	bus stop
SUBIR/BAJAR	enter/exit
MARCAR BOLETO	stamp your ticket

The bus service in Mexico is extensive, since air travel is expensive and the passenger rail service is not well developed. For local service within a town or city, you pay as you board the bus. The fare depends on how far you travel.

Buses are called by different names: **camión**, **micro**, **pesera**. The **camión** is the public bus. **Micro** and **pesera** are privately operated; the **micro** is larger than the **pesera**, but not as large as the **camión**.

The new **Metrobus** system works very well as it uses exclusive lanes and electronic tickets sold in vending machines. This bus system currently goes along the longest avenue in Mexico City and crosses the city north to south.

Subway [Underground]

Where's the subway [underground] station?	**¿Dónde está la estación del metro?** dohn•deh ehs•tah lah ehs•tah•seeyohn dehl meh•troh
A map, please.	**Un mapa, por favor.** oon mah•pah pohr fah•bohr
Which line for...?	**¿Qué línea tengo que tomar para...?** keh lee•neh•ah tehn•goh keh toh•mahr pah•rah...
Do I have to transfer [change]?	**¿Tengo que transbordar?** tehn•goh keh trahnz•bohr•dahr
Is this the subway [train] to...?	**¿Éste es el metro para...?** ehs•teh ehs ehl meh•troh pah•rah...
Where are we?	**¿Dónde estamos?** dohn•deh ehs•tah•mohs

▶For ticketing, see page 20.

Mexico City, Guadalajara and Monterrey have **metro** (subway) systems. Subways in Mexico are easy to use and reasonably priced. All systems operate on a one-way, per-ride basis. To enter the subway system, slip your ticket through the slot in the turnstile. Tickets can be bought at the station's ticket office.

Boat and Ferry

When is the ferry to…?	**¿Cuándo sale el transbordador a…?** kwahn•doh sah•leh ehl trahnz•boh•dah•dohr ah…
Can I take my car?	**¿Puedo llevar el coche?** pweh•doh yeh•bahr ehl koh•cheh

▶For ticketing, see page 20.

You May See…

BOTE SALVAVIDAS	life boat
CHALECO SALVAVIDAS	life jacket

Ferries are not usually used on a daily basis by the local Mexicans, as they are located mainly at tourist attractions.

There are ferries traveling from Cozumel Island to Playa del Carmen, from Isla Mujeres to Cancun and from Mazatlán to La Paz in the Gulf of California.

Bicycle and Motorcycle

I'd like to rent [hire]…	**Quiero rentar…** keeyeh•roh rrehn•tahr…
– a bicycle	**– una bicicleta** oo•nah bee•see•kleh•tah
– a moped	**– una motoneta** oo•nah moh•toh•neh•tah
– a motorcycle	**– una motocicleta** oo•nah moh•toh•see•kleh•tah
How much per *day/week*?	**¿Cuánto cuesta por *día/semana*?** kwahn•toh kwehs•tah pohr *dee•ah/ seh•mah•nah*
Can I have a *helmet/lock*?	**¿Puede darme un *casco/candado*?** pweh•deh dahr•meh oon *kahs•koh/kahn•dah•doh*

Taxi

Where can I get a taxi?	**¿Dónde puedo tomar un taxi?** dohn•deh pweh•doh toh•mahr oon tah•xee
Do you have the number for a taxi?	**¿Tiene el número de algún sitio de taxi?** teeyeh•neh ehl noo•meh•roh deh ahl•goon see•tee•oh deh tah•xee
I'd like a taxi *now/ for tomorrow at...*	**Quiero un taxi *ahora/para mañana a la(s)...*** keeyeh•roh oon tah•xee *ah•oh•rah/ pah•rah mah•nyah•nah ah lah(s)...*
Pick me up at (place/time)...	**Pase por mí *en/a la(s)...*** pah•seh porh mee *ehn/ah lah(s)...*

▶For when to use **la** or **las**, see page 174.

I'm going to...	**Voy...** boy...
– this address	**– a esta dirección** ah ehs•tah dee•rehk•seeyohn
– the airport	**– al aeropuerto** ahl ah•eh•roh•pwehr•toh
– the train [railway] station	**– a la estación del tren** ah lah ehs•tah•seeyohn dehl trehn
I'm late.	**Voy retrasado.** vohee rreh•trah•sah•doh
Can you drive *faster/slower*?	**¿Puede ir más *deprisa/despacio*?** pweh•deh eer mahs *deh•pree•sah/ dehs•pah•seeyoh*
Stop/Wait here.	***Pare/Espere* aquí.** *pah•reh/ehs•peh•reh* ah•kee
How much?	**¿Cuánto es?** kwahn•toh ehs
You said it would cost...	**Dijo que costaría...** dee•khoh keh kohs•tah•ree•ah...
Keep the change.	**Quédese con el cambio.** keh•deh•seh kohn ehl kahm•beeyoh

In some Spanish-speaking countries **coger** means to get or catch, as in: **¿Dónde puedo coger un taxi?** (Where can I catch a taxi?) However, in Mexico, **coger** is a vulgarity for "to have sex". Travelers to Mexico should always use **tomar** or **abordar** (**¿Dónde puedo tomar un taxi?**).

You May Hear...

¿Para donde va? pah·rah dohn·deh vah	Where to?
¿Cuál es la dirección? kwahl ehs lah dee·rehk·seeyohn	What's the address?

In major Mexican cities, taxis are reasonably priced. When entering the taxi, make sure the meter is turned on; it should register a base fare when the trip begins. The fare is then increased per kilometer traveled.

Be sure to hail a licensed taxi; these are white with a red horizontal strip at the side of the car. You can also call ahead for licensed taxi service; these may be more expensive but are safe.

Car

Car Rental [Hire]

Where can I rent a car?	**¿Dónde puedo rentar un auto?** dohn·deh pweh·doh rrehn·tahr oon aw·toh
I'd like...	**Quiero...** keeyeh·roh...
– a *cheap/small* car	**– un auto *barato/compacto*** oon aw·toh *bah·rah·toh/kohm·pahk·toh*
– an automatic/ a manual	**– un auto *automático/con transmisión manual*** oon aw·toh *aw·toh·mah·tee·koh/kohn trahnz·mee·seeyohn mah·noo·ahl*

– air conditioning	**– un auto con aire acondicionado** oon aw•toh kohn ayee•reh ah•kohn•dee•seeyoh•nah•doh
– a car seat	**– un asiento de niño** oon ah•seeyehn•toh deh nee•nyoh
How much...?	**¿Cuánto cobran...?** kwahn•toh koh•brahn...
– per *day/week*	**– por *día/semana*** pohr *dee•ah/ seh•mah•nah*
– for...days	**– por...días** pohr...dee•ahs
– per kilometer	**– por kilómetro** pohr kee•loh•meh•troh
– for unlimited mileage	**– por kilometraje ilimitado** pohr kee•loh•meh•trah•kheh ee•lee•mee•tah•doh
– with insurance	**– con el seguro** kohn ehl seh•goo•roh
Are there any discounts?	**¿Ofrecen algún descuento?** oh•freh•sehn ahl•goon dehs•kwehn•toh

You May Hear...

¿Tiene licencia de conducir internacional? teeyeh•neh lee•sehn•seeyah deh kohn•doo•seer een•tehr•nah•seeyoh•nahl	Do you have an international driver's license?
Su pasaporte, por favor. soo pah•sah•pohr•teh pohr fah•bohr	Your passport, please.
¿Quiere seguro? keeyeh•reh seh•goo•roh	Do you want insurance?
Necesitaré un depósito. neh•seh•see•tah•reh oon deh•poh•see•toh	I'll need a deposit.
Firme aquí. feer•meh ah•kee	Sign here.

Gas [Petrol] Station

Where's the gas [petrol] station?	**¿Dónde está la gasolinera?** dohn·deh ehs·tah lah gah·soh·lee·neh·rah
Fill it up.	**Lleno.** yeh·noh
…liters, please.	**…litros, por favor.** …lee·trohs pohr fah·bohr
I'll pay *in cash/by credit card.*	**Voy a pagar *en efectivo/con tarjeta de crédito.*** boy ah pah·gahr *ehn eh·fehk·tee·boh/ kohn tahr·kheh·tah deh kreh·dee·toh*

You May See…

MAGNA SIN	regular
MAGNA PREMIUM	super
DIÉSEL	diesel

Asking Directions

Is this the way to…?	**¿Es ésta la ruta a…?** ehs ehs·tah lah rroo·tah ah…
How far is it to…?	**¿A qué distancia está…?** ah keh dees·tahn·seeyah ehs·tah…
Where's…?	**¿Dónde está…?** dohn·deh ehs·tah…
– this address	**– esta dirección** ehs·tah dee·rehk·seeyohn
– the highway [motorway]	**– la autopista** lah aw·toh·pees·tah
– …Street	**– la calle…** lah kah·yeh…
Can you show me on the map?	**¿Me lo puede indicar en el mapa?** meh loh pweh·deh een·dee·kahr ehn ehl mah·pah
I'm lost.	**Me perdí.** meh pehr·dee

You May Hear...

de frente deh frehn•teh	straight ahead
a la izquierda ah lah ees•keeyehr•dah	left
a la derecha ah lah deh•reh•chah	right
***en/doblando* la esquina** *ehn/doh•blahn•doh* lah ehs•kee•nah	*on/around* the corner
frente a frehn•teh ah	opposite
detrás de deh•trahs deh	behind
al lado de ahl lah•doh deh	next to
después de dehs•pwehs deh	after
al *norte/sur* ahl *nohr•teh/soor*	north/south
al *este/oeste* ahl *ehs•teh/oh•ehs•teh*	east/west
en el semáforo en ehl seh•mah•foh•roh	at the traffic light
en el cruce en ehl kroo•seh	at the intersection

Parking

Can I park here?	**¿Puedo estacionarme aquí?** pweh•doh es•tah•seeyoh•nahr•meh ah•kee
Where's the *parking garage/parking lot [car park]*?	**¿Dónde está el *garaje/estacionamiento*?** dohn•deh ehs•tah ehl *gah•rah•kheh/ es•tah•seeyoh•nah•meeyehn•toh*
How much...?	**¿Cuánto cobran...?** kwahn•toh koh•brahn...
– per hour	**– por hora** pohr oh•rah
– per day	**– por día** pohr dee•ah
– for overnight	**– por la noche** pohr lah noh•cheh

Parking is permitted on most streets. Some areas offer restricted parking with parking meters. In zones where parking is not allowed you may see **PROHIBIDO ESTACIONARSE** (no parking) or sometimes you will find a yellow line on the curb.

Traffic authorities may tow your vehicle for illegal parking and payment of fines (with a credit or debit card) on the spot may be required.

Breakdown and Repairs

My car *broke down/ won't start.*	**El auto *se descompuso/no arranca.*** ehl aw•toh *seh des•kohm•poo•soh/noh ah•rrahn•kah*
Can you fix it (today)?	**¿Puede arreglarlo (hoy mismo)?** pweh•deh ah•rreh•glahr•loh (oy meez•moh)
When will it be ready?	**¿Cuándo estará listo?** kwahn•doh ehs•tah•rah lees•toh
How much?	**¿Cuánto es?** kwahn•toh ehs

Accidents

There was an accident.	**Hubo un accidente.** oo•boh oon ahk•see•dehn•teh
Call *an ambulance/ the police.*	**Llame a *una ambulancia/la policía.*** yah•meh ah *oo•nah ahm•boo•lahn•seeyah/ lah poh•lee•see•ah*

You May See...

PROHIBIDO REBASAR — no passing zone

ALTO — stop

DOBLE CIRCULACIÓN — two-way street

CEDA EL PASO — yield [give way]

SÓLO VUELTA A LA IZQUIERDA — turn left

PROHIBIDO ESTACIONARSE — no parking

PROHIBIDA LA VUELTA A LA DERECHA — no right turn

LÍMITE MÁXIMO DE VELOCIDAD — maximum speed limit

Accommodations

Essential

Can you recommend a hotel?	**¿Puede recomendarme un hotel?** pweh•deh rreh•koh•mehn•dahr•meh oon oh•tehl
I have a reservation.	**Tengo una reserva.** tehn•goh oo•nah rreh•sehr•bah
My name is…	**Me llamo…** meh yah•moh…
Do you have a room…?	**¿Tienen habitaciones…?** teeyeh•nehn ah•bee•tah•seeyoh•nehs…
– for *one/two*	**– sencillas/dobles** sehn•see•yahs/doh•blehs
– with a bathroom	**– con baño** kohn bah•nyoh
– with air conditioning	**– con aire acondicionado** kohn ayee•reh ah•kohn•dee•seeyoh•nah•doh
For…	**Para…** pah•rah…
– tonight	**– esta noche** ehs•tah noh•cheh
– two nights	**– dos noches** dohs noh•chehs
– one week	**– una semana** oo•nah seh•mah•nah
How much?	**¿Cuánto es?** kwahn•toh ehs
Is there anything cheaper?	**¿Hay alguna tarifa más barata?** aye ahl•goo•nah tah•ree•fah mahs bah•rah•tah
When's check-out?	**¿A qué hora hay que desocupar la habitación?** ah keh oh•rah aye keh deh•soh•koo•pahr lah ah•bee•tah•seeyohn
Can I leave this in the safe?	**¿Puedo dejar esto en la caja fuerte?** pweh•doh deh•khahr ehs•toh ehn lah kah•khah fwehr•teh

Can I leave my bags?	**¿Podría dejar mi equipaje?** poh•dree•ah deh•khahr mee eh•kee•pah•kheh
Can I have *the bill/ a receipt*?	**¿Me da *la factura/un comprobante*?** meh dah *lah fahk•too•rah/oon kohm•proh•bahn•teh*
I'll pay *in cash/by credit card.*	**Voy a pagar *en efectivo/con tarjeta de crédito.*** boy ah pah•gahr *ehn eh•fehk•tee•boh/kohn tahr•kheh•tah deh kreh•dee•toh*

If you didn't reserve accommodations before your trip, visit the local **Oficina de Turismo** (Tourist Information Office) or any local travel agency for recommendations on places to stay.

Finding Lodging

Can you recommend a hotel?	**¿Puede recomendarme un hotel?** pweh•deh rreh•koh•mehn•dahr•meh oon oh•tehl
What is it near?	**¿Qué hay cerca?** keh aye sehr•kah
How do I get there?	**¿Cómo llego?** koh•moh yeh•goh

A variety of accommodations is available in Mexico. Hotels are rated from one to five stars, with five stars being the most expensive and having the most amenities. Other unique accommodations in Mexico include spas, resorts, hostels and lodges.

In order to book a room online at a hotel or resort visit the **Secretaría de Turismo** webpage.

▶For useful websites, see page 185.

At the Hotel

I have a reservation.	**Tengo una reserva.** tehn•goh oo•nah rreh•sehr•bah
My name is…	**Me llamo…** meh yah•moh…
Do you have a room…?	**¿Tiene una habitación…?** teeyeh•neh oo•nah ah•bee•tah•seeyohn…
– for *one/two*	**– sencilla/doble** sehn•see•yah/doh•bleh
– with a *bathroom [toilet]/shower*	**– con *un baño/una regadera*** kohn *oon bah•nyoh/oo•nah rreh•gah•deh•rah*
– with air conditioning	**– con aire acondicionado** kohn ayee•reh ah•kohn•dee•seeyoh•nah•doh
– with a *single/double* bed	**– con una *cama/cama matrimonial*** kohn oo•nah *kah•mah/kah•mah mah•tree•moh•neeyahl*
– that's *smoking/non-smoking*	**– para *fumadores/no fumadores*** pah•rah *foo•mah•doh•rehs/noh foo•mah•doh•rehs*

For…	**Para…** pah·rah…
– tonight	**– esta noche** ehs·tah noh·cheh
– two nights	**– dos noches** dohs noh·chehs
– a week	**– una semana** oo·nah seh·mah·nah

▶For numbers, see page 178.

Does the hotel have…?	**¿El hotel tiene…?** ehl oh·tehl teeyeh·neh…
– a computer	**– una computadora** oo·nah kohm·poo·tah·doh·rah
– an elevator [a lift]	**– un elevador** oon eh·leh·bah·dohr
– a gym	**– un gimnasio** oon kheem·nah·seeyoh
– (wireless) internet service	**– acceso (inalámbrico) a Internet** ahk·seh·soh (een·ah·lahm·bree·koh) ah een·tehr·neht
– a pool	**– una alberca** oo·nah ahl·behr·kah
– room service	**– servicio a la habitación** sehr·bee·seeyoh ah lah ah·bee·tah·seeyohn
I need…	**Necesito…** neh·seh·see·toh…
– an extra bed	**– otra cama** oh·trah kah·mah
– a cot	**– un catre** oon kah·treh
– a crib	**– una cuna** oo·nah koo·nah

You May Hear…

Su *pasaporte/tarjeta de crédito*, por favor. soo *pah·sah·pohr·teh/ tahr·kheh·tah deh kreh·dee·toh* pohr fah·bohr	Your *passport/ credit card*, please.
Llene este formulario. yeh·neh ehs·teh fohr·moo·lah·reeyoh	Fill out this form.
Firme aquí. feer·meh ah·kee	Sign here.

Price

How much per *night/week*?	**¿Cuánto cuesta por *noche/semana*?** kwahn·toh kwehs·tah pohr *noh·cheh/seh·mah·nah*
Does that include *breakfast/sales tax [VAT]*?	**¿El precio incluye el *desayuno/IVA*?** ehl preh·seeyoh een·kloo·yeh ehl *deh·sah·yoo·noh/ee·bah*

Questions

Can I see the room?	**¿Puedo ver la habitación?** pweh·doh behr lah ah·bee·tah·seeyohn
Where's...?	**¿Dónde está...?** dohn·deh ehs·tah...
– the bar	**– el bar** ehl bahr
– the bathroom [toilet]	**– el baño** ehl bah·nyoh
– the elevator [lift]	**– el elevador** ehl eh·leh·bah·dohr
Can I have...?	**¿Puede darme...?** pweh·deh dahr·meh...
– a blanket	**– una cobija** oo·nah coh·bee·khah
– an iron	**– una plancha** oo·nah plahn·chah
– a pillow	**– una almohada** oo·nah ahl·moh·ah·dah
– soap	**– jabón** khah·bohn
– toilet paper	**– papel higiénico** pah·pehl ee·kheeyeh·nee·koh
– a towel	**– una toalla** oo·nah toh·ah·yah
Do you have an adapter for this?	**¿Tiene un adaptador para esto?** teeyeh·neh oon ah·dahp·tah·dohr pah·rah ehs·toh
How do I turn on the lights?	**¿Cómo prendo las luces?** koh·moh prehn·doh lahs loo·sehs
Can you wake me at...?	**¿Podría despertarme a la/las...?** poh·dree·ah dehs·pehr·tahr·meh ah lah/lahs...

▶For when to use **la** or **las**, see page 174.

Can I leave this in the safe?	**¿Puedo dejar esto en la caja fuerte?** pweh·doh deh·khahr ehs·toh ehn lah kah·khah fwehr·teh
Can I have my things from the safe?	**¿Podría darme mis cosas de la caja fuerte?** poh·dree·ah dahr·meh mees koh·sahs deh lah kah·khah fwehr·teh
Is there *mail [post]/ a message* for me?	**¿Hay *correo/algún mensaje* para mí?** aye *koh·rreh·oh/ahl·goon mehn·sah·kheh* pah·rah mee

When asking for a public restroom, say **¿Dónde está el baño?** or **¿Dónde están los sanitarios?** Most speakers of Mexican Spanish will use **baño**, but **sanitarios** will be used on signs.

You May See...

EMPUJAR/JALAR	push/pull
BAÑO/SANITARIOS	bathroom/restroom [toilet]
REGADERA	shower
ELEVADOR	elevator [lift]
ESCALERAS	stairs
LAVANDERÍA	laundry
NO MOLESTAR	do not disturb
PUERTA DE INCENDIOS	fire door
SALIDA (DE EMERGENCIA)	(emergency) exit
SERVICIO DE DESPERTADOR	wake-up call

Problems

There's a problem. **Hay un problema.** aye oon proh•bleh•mah

I lost my *key/key card.* **Perdí la *llave/tarjeta electrónica.*** pehr•dee lah *yah•beh/tahr•kheh•tah eh•lehk•troh•nee•kah*

I'm locked out of the room. **Dejé la llave dentro de la habitación.** deh•kheh lah yah•beh dehn•troh deh lah ah•bee•tah•seeyohn

There's no *hot water/toilet paper.* **No hay *agua caliente/papel higiénico.*** no aye *ah•gwah kah•leeyehn•teh/pah•pehl ee•kheeyeh•nee•koh*

The room is dirty. **La habitación está sucia.** lah ah•bee•tah•seeyohn ehs•tah soo•seeyah

There are bugs in the room. **Hay insectos en la habitación.** aye een•sehk•tohs ehn lah ah•bee•tah•seeyohn

...doesn't work. **...no funciona.** ...no foon•seeyoh•nah

Can you fix...? **¿Pueden arreglar...?** pweh•dehn ah•rreh•glahr...

– the air conditioning **– el aire acondicionado** ehl ayee•reh ah•kohn•dee•seeyoh•nah•doh

– the fan **– el ventilador** ehl behn•tee•lah•dohr

– the heat [heating] **– la calefacción** lah kah•leh•fahk•seeyohn

– the light **– la luz** lah loos

– the TV **– la televisión** lah teh•leh•bee•seeyohn

– the toilet **– el excusado** ehl ehx•koo•sah•doh

I'd like another room. **Quiero otra habitación.** keeyeh•roh oh•trah ah•bee•tah•seeyohn

Voltage in Mexico for electrical appliances is 110 volts, 60 Hz. A converter and/or an adapter may be needed for foreign appliances.

Check-out

When's check-out?	**¿A qué hora hay que desocupar la habitación?** ah keh oh•rah aye keh dehs•oh•koo•pahr lah ah•bee•tah•seeyohn
Can I leave my bags here until…?	**¿Puedo dejar mis maletas aquí hasta…?** pweh•doh deh•khahr mees mah•leh•tahs ah•kee ahs•tah…
Can I have *an itemized bill/ a receipt*?	**¿Puede darme *una factura detallada/ un comprobante*?** pweh•deh dahr•meh *oo•nah fahk•too•rah deh•tah•yah•dah/oon kohm•proh•bahn•teh*
I think there's a mistake.	**Creo que hay un error.** kreh•oh keh aye oon eh•rrohr
I made… phone calls.	**Hice…llamadas.** ee•seh… yah•mah•dahs
I took…from the mini-bar.	**Tomé…del minibar.** toh•meh… dehl mee•nee•bar
I'll pay *in cash/by credit card.*	**Voy a pagar *en efectivo/con tarjeta de crédito.*** boy ah pah•gahr *ehn eh•fehk•tee•boh/ kohn tahr•kheh•tah deh kreh•dee•toh*

Tipping the porter in hotels is customary in Mexico. The amount varies based on the type of hotel. The more exclusive the hotel, the larger the tip should be.

Renting

I reserved *an apartment/room.*	**Reservé *un departamento/una habitación.*** rreh·sehr·beh *oon deh·pahr·tah·mehn·toh/oo·nah ah·bee·tah·seeyohn*
My name is…	**Me llamo…** meh yah·moh…
Can I have the *key/key card?*	**¿Puede darme la *llave/tarjeta electrónica?*** *pweh·deh dahr·meh lah yah·beh/tahr·keh·tah eh·lehk·troh·nee·kah*
Are there…?	**¿Hay…?** aye…
– dishes	**– platos** plah·tohs
– pillows	**– almohadas** ahl·moh·ah·dahs
– sheets	**– sábanas** sah·bah·nahs
– towels	**– toallas** toh·ah·yahs
– utensils	**– cubiertos** koo·beeyehr·tohs
When do I put out the trash [rubbish]?	**¿Cuándo saco la basura?** kwahn·doh sah·koh lah bah·soo·rah
…is broken.	**…está roto♂/rota♀.** …ehs·tah rroh·toh♂/rroh·tah♀
How does… work?	**¿Cómo funciona…?** koh·moh foon·seeyoh·nah…
– the air conditioner	**– el aire acondicionado** ehl ayee·reh ah·kohn·dee·seeyoh·nah·doh
– the dishwasher	**– el lavaplatos** ehl lah·bah·plah·tohs
– the freezer	**– el congelador** ehl kohn·kheh·lah·dohr
– the heater	**– la calefacción** lah kah·leh·fahk·seeyohn
– the microwave	**– el microondas** ehl mee·kroh·ohn·dahs
– the refrigerator	**– el refrigerador** ehl rreh·free·kheh·rah·dohr
– the stove	**– el horno** ehl ohr·noh
– the washing machine	**– la lavadora** lah lah·bah·doh·rah

Household Items

I need...	**Necesito...** neh•seh•see•toh...
– an adapter	**– un adaptador** oon ah•dahp•tah•dohr
– aluminum [kitchen] foil	**– papel aluminio** pah•pehl ah•loo•mee•neeyoh
– a bottle opener	**– un destapador** oon dehs•tah•pah•dohr
– a broom	**– una escoba** oo•nah ehs•koh•bah
– a can opener	**– un abrelatas** oon ah•breh•lah•tahs
– cleaning supplies	**– productos de limpieza** proh•dook•tohs deh leem•peeyeh•sah
– a corkscrew	**– un sacacorchos** oon sah•kah•kohr•chohs
– detergent	**– detergente** deh•tehr•khehn•teh
– dishwashing liquid	**– líquido lavaplatos** lee•kee•doh lah•bah•plah•tohs
– garbage [rubbish] bags	**– bolsas de basura** bohl•sahs deh bah•soo•rah
– a lightbulb	**– un foco** oon foh•koh
– matches	**– cerillos** seh•ree•yohs
– a mop	**– un trapeador** oon trah•peh•ah•dohr
– napkins	**– servilletas** sehr•bee•yeh•tahs
– paper towels	**– toallas de papel** toh•ah•yahs deh pah•pehl
– plastic wrap [cling film]	**– plástico transparente** plahs•tee•koh trahns•pah•rehn•teh
– a plunger	**– un destapador** oon desh•tah•pah•dohr
– scissors	**– tijeras** tee•kheh•rahs
– a vacuum cleaner	**– una aspiradora** oo•nah ahs•pee•rah•doh•rah

▶For dishes and utensils, see page 69.

▶For oven temperatures, see page 184.

Hostel

Is there a bed available?	**¿Hay camas disponibles?** ahy kah•mahs dees•poh•nee•blehs
Can I have...?	**¿Me puede dar...?** meh pweh•deh dahr...
– a *single/double* room	**– una habitación *sencilla/doble*** oo•nah ah•bee•tah•seeyohn *sehn•see•yah/doh•bleh*
– a blanket	**– una cobija** oo•nah koh•bee•khah
– a pillow	**– una almohada** oo•nah ahl•moh•ah•dah
– sheets	**– sábanas** sah•bah•nahs
– a towel	**– una toalla** oo•nah toh•ah•yah
When do you lock up?	**¿A qué hora cierran las puertas?** ah keh oh•rah seeyeh•rrahn lahs pwehr•tahs
Do I need a membership card?	**¿Necesito una tarjeta de socio?** neh•seh•see•toh oo•nah tahr•kheh•tah de soh•seeyoh
Here's my International Student Card.	**Aquí tiene mi credencial internacional de estudiante.** ah•kee teeyeh•neh mee kreh•dehn•seeahl een•tehr•nah•seeyoh•nahl deh ehs•too•deeyahn•teh

There are many hostels in Mexico, so finding an inexpensive place to stay should be easy. Hostels offer dormitory-style rooms and, sometimes, private or semi-private rooms. Some offer private bathrooms, though most have shared facilities.

There is usually a self-service kitchen on site. Reservations are recommended in advance in larger cities and popular destinations during the tourist season.

▶For useful websites, see page 185.

Camping

Can I camp here?	**¿Puedo acampar aquí?** pweh·doh ah·kahm·pahr ah·kee
Where's the campsite?	**¿Dónde está el campamento?** dohn·deh ehs·tah ehl kahm·pah·mehn·toh
What is the charge per *day/week*?	**¿Cuánto cobran por *día/semana*?** kwahn·toh koh·brahn pohr *dee·ah/ seh·mah·nah*
Are there...?	**¿Hay...?** aye...
– cooking facilities	**– instalaciones para cocinar** eens·tah·lah·seeyoh·nehs pah·rah koh·see·nahr
– electric outlets	**– enchufes eléctricos** ehn·choo·fehs eh·lehk·tree·kohs
– laundry facilities	**– servicio de lavandería** sehr·bee·seeyoh deh lah·bahn·deh·ree·ah
– showers	**– regaderas** rreh·gah·deh·rahs
– tents for rent [hire]	**– renta de tiendas de campaña** rrehn·tah deh teeyehn·dahs deh kahm·pah·nya
Where can I empty the chemical toilet?	**¿Dónde puedo vaciar el excusado químico?** dohn·deh pweh·doh bah·seeyahr ehl ehx·koo·sah·doh kee·mee·koh

You May See...

AGUA POTABLE	drinking water
PROHIBIDO ACAMPAR	no camping
PROHIBIDO HACER *PARRILLADAS/HOGUERAS*	no *fires/ barbecues*

▶For household items, see page 47.

▶For dishes and utensils, see page 69.

Internet and Communications

Essential

Where's an internet cafe?
¿Dónde hay un café Internet? dohn·deh aye oon cah·feh een·tehr·neht

Can I *access the internet/check e-mail*?
¿Puedo *entrar a Internet/revisar el correo electrónico*? pweh·doh *ehn·trahr ah een·tehr·neht/reh·bee·sahr ehl koh·rreh·oh eh·lehk·troh·nee·koh*

How much per (half) hour?
¿Cuánto cuesta por (media) hora? kwahn·toh kwehs·tah pohr (meh·deeyah) oh·rah

How do I *connect/log on*?
¿Cómo *me conecto/inicio la sesión*? koh·moh *meh koh·nehk·toh/ee·nee·seeyoh lah seh·seeyohn*

A phone card, please.
Una tarjeta de teléfono, por favor. oo·nah tahr·kheh·tah deh teh·leh·foh·noh pohr fah·bohr

Can I have your phone number?
¿Me puede dar su número de teléfono? meh pweh·deh dahr soo noo·meh·roh deh teh·leh·foh·noh

Here's my *number/e-mail address*.
Este es mi número/Esta es mi dirección de correo electrónico. ehs·teh ehs mee noo·meh·roh/ ehs·tah ehs mee dee·rehk·seeyohn deh koh·rreh·oh eh·lehk·troh·nee koh

Call me.
Llámeme. yah·meh·meh

E-mail me.
Envíeme un correo electrónico. ehn·bee·eh·meh oon koh·rreh·oh eh·lehk·troh·nee·koh

Hello. This is...
Hola. Soy... oh·lah soy...

Can I speak to...?
¿Puedo hablar con...? pweh·doh ah·blahr kohn...

Can you repeat that?	**¿Puede repetir eso?** pweh•deh rreh•peh•teer eh•soh
I'll call back later.	**Llamaré más tarde.** yah•mah•reh mahs tahr•deh
Bye.	**Adiós.** ah•deeyohs
Where's the post office?	**¿Dónde está la oficina de correos?** dohn•deh ehs•tah lah oh•fee•see•nah deh koh•rreh•ohs
I'd like to send this to…	**Quiero mandar esto a…** keeyeh•roh mahn•dahr ehs•toh ah…

Computer, Internet and E-mail

Where's an internet cafe?	**¿Dónde hay un café Internet?** dohn•deh aye oon cah•feh een•tehr•neht
Does it have wireless internet?	**¿Tiene Internet inalámbrico?** teeyeh•neh een•tehr•neht een•ah•lahm•bree•koh
How do I turn the computer *on/off*?	**¿Cómo *prendo/apago* la computadora?** koh•moh *prehn•doh/ah•pah•goh* lah kohm•poo•tah•doh•rah
Can I…?	**¿Puedo…?** pweh•doh…
– access the internet	**– entrar a Internet** ehn•trahr ah een•tehr•neht
– check e-mail	**– revisar el correo electrónico** rreh•bee•sahr ehl koh•rreh•oh eh•lehk•troh•nee•koh
– print	**– imprimir** eem•pree•meer
How much per (half) hour?	**¿Cuánto cuesta por (media) hora?** kwahn•toh kwehs•tah pohr (meh•deeyah) oh•rah

How do I...?	**¿Cómo...?** koh·moh...
– *connect/ disconnect*	**– me *conecto/desconecto*** meh *koh·nehk·toh/dehs·koh·nehk·toh*
– log *on/off*	**– *inicio/cierro* la sesión** *ee·nee·seeyoh/ seeyeh·rroh* lah seh·seeyohn
– type this symbol	**– escribo este símbolo** ehs·kree·boh ehs·teh seem·boh·loh
What's your e-mail?	**¿Cuál es su dirección de correo electrónico?** kwahl ehs soo dee·rehk·seeyohn deh koh·rreh·oh eh·lehk·troh·nee·koh
My e-mail is...	**Mi dirección de correo electrónico es...** mee dee·rehk·seeyohn deh koh·rreh·oh eh·lehk·troh·nee·koh ehs...

You May See...

CERRAR	close
BORRAR	delete
CORREO ELECTRÓNICO	e-mail
SALIR	exit
AYUDA	help
MENSAJERO INSTANTÁNEO	instant messenger
INTERNET	internet
NUEVO (MENSAJE)	new (message)
PRENDER/APAGAR	on/off
ABRIR	open
IMPRIMIR	print
GUARDAR	save
ENVIAR	send
NOMBRE DE USUARIO/CONTRASEÑA	username/password
INTERNET INALÁMBRICO	wireless internet

There are many internet cafes throughout Mexico, especially in bigger cities. These are very popular, as not everyone has personal access to the internet. You usually pay a set fee per hour.

Many restaurants, cafes and hotels have wireless internet service.

Phone

A *phone card/ prepaid phone*, please.	***Una tarjeta de teléfono/Un teléfono prepago*, por favor.** *oo•nah tahr•kheh•tah deh teh•leh•foh•noh/oon teh•leh•foh•noh preh•pah•goh* pohr fah•bohr
How much?	**¿Cuánto es?** kwahn•toh ehs
My phone doesn't work here.	**Mi teléfono no sirve aquí.** mee teh•leh•foh•noh noh seer•beh ah•kee
What's the *area code/country code* for...?	**¿Cuál es el *código local/código de país* para...?** kwahl ehs ehl *koh•dee•goh loh•kahl/ koh•dee•goh deh pah•ees* pah•rah ...
What's the number for Information?	**¿Cuál es el número de información?** kwahl ehs ehl noo•meh•roh deh een•fohr•mah•seeyohn
I'd like the number for...	**Necesito el número de teléfono de...** neh•seh•see•toh ehl noo•meh•roh deh teh•leh•foh•noh deh...
Can I have your number?	**¿Me puede dar su número de teléfono?** meh pweh•deh dahr soo noo•meh•roh deh teh•leh•foh•noh
Here's my number.	**Este es mi número.** ehs•teh ehs mee noo•meh•roh

▶For numbers, see page 178.

Please call me.	**Llámeme, por favor.** yah•meh•meh pohr fah•bohr
Please text me.	**Envíeme un mensaje de texto, por favor.** ehn•beeyeh•meh oon mehn•sah•kheh deh tehx•toh pohr fah•bohr
I'll call you.	**Lo♂/La♀ llamaré.** loh♂/lah♀ yah•mah•reh
I'll text you.	**Le enviaré un mensaje de texto.** leh ehn•bee•ah•reh oon mehn•sah•kheh deh tehx•toh

On the Phone

Hello. This is...	**Hola. Soy...** oh·lah soy...
Can I speak to...?	**¿Puedo hablar con...?** pweh·doh ah·blahr kohn...
Extension...	**Extensión...** ehx·tehn·seeyohn...
Speak *louder/more slowly*, please.	**Hable más *alto/despacio*, por favor.** ah·bleh mahs *ahl·toh/dehs·pah·seeyoh* pohr fah·bohr
Can you repeat that?	**¿Puede repetir eso?** pweh·deh rreh·peh·teer eh·soh
I'll call back later.	**Llamaré más tarde.** yah·mah·reh mahs tahr·deh
Bye.	**Adiós.** ah·deeyohs

▶For business travel, see page 152.

Public phones in Mexico are coin or card operated, but due to the popularity and availability of cell phones, they are becoming a rare sight. Phone cards can be purchased at newsstands and supermarkets. There is cell phone coverage in most of the country; GSM is the most widely used system.

For international calls, prepaid calling cards are the most economical and are available at most newsstands. You can also make your long-distance calls at **centros de negocios** (business centers). These also offer internet, fax and wireless phone-charging services at reasonable prices. Calling internationally from your hotel may be convenient, but the rates can be very expensive. To call the U.S. or Canada from Mexico, dial 00 + 1 + area code + phone number. To call the U.K. from Mexico, dial 00 + 44 + area code (minus the first 0) + phone number.

¿Quién habla? keeyehn ah•blah — Who's calling?

Espere. ehs•peh•reh — Hold on.

Le comunico. leh coh•muh•nee•coh — I'll put you through.

No está. noh ehs•tah — He/She is not here.

No puede atenderlo♂/atenderla♀ en este momento. noh pweh•deh ah•tehn•dehr•loh♂/ ah•tehn•dehr•lah♀ ehn ehs•teh moh•mehn•toh — He/She can't come to the phone.

¿Quiere dejarle un mensaje? keeyeh•reh deh•khahr•leh oon mehn•sah•kheh — Would you like to leave a message?

Vuelva a llamar *más tarde/en diez minutos.* bwehl•bah ah yah•mahr *mahs tahr•deh/ehn deeyehs mee•noo•tohs* — Call back *later/in 10 minutes.*

¿Quiere que le devuelva la llamada? keeyeh•reh keh leh deh•bwehl•bah lah yah•mah•dah — Can he/she call you back?

¿Me da su número? meh dah soo noo•meh•roh — What's your number?

Fax

Can I *send/receive* a fax here? — **¿Puedo *enviar/recibir* un fax aquí?** pweh•doh *ehn•bee•ahr/reh•see•beer* oon fahx ah•kee

What's the fax number? — **¿Cuál es el número de fax?** kwahl ehs ehl noo•meh•roh deh fahx

Please fax this to… — **Por favor envíe este fax a…** pohr fah•bohr ehn•bee•eh ehs•teh fahx ah…

Post Office

Where's the *post office/mailbox [postbox]*?	**¿Dónde está *la oficina/el buzón* de correos?** dohn•deh ehs•tah *lah oh•fee•see•nah/ehl boo•sohn* deh koh•rreh•ohs
A stamp for this *postcard/letter* to...	**Una estampilla para esta *postal/carta* a...** oo•nah ehs•tahm•pee•yah pah•rah ehs•tah *pohs•tahl/kahr•tah* ah...
How much?	**¿Cuánto es?** kwahn•toh ehs
I want to send this package *by airmail/ express*.	**Quiero mandar este paquete por correo *aéreo/urgente*.** keeyeh•roh mahn•dahr ehs•teh pah•keh•teh pohr koh•rreh•oh *ah•eh•reh•oh/ oor•khen•teh*
A receipt, please.	**Un comprobante, por favor.** oon kohn•proh•bahn•teh pohr fah•bohr

You May Hear...

Llene la declaración aduanal. yeh•neh lah deh•klah•rah•seeyohn ah•dwah•nahl	Fill out the customs declaration form.
¿Qué valor tiene? keh bah•lohr teeyeh•neh	What's the value?
¿Qué hay dentro? keh aye dehn•troh	What's inside?

Las Oficinas de Correos (post offices) offer standard postal services.

The Mexican Post Office offers a service called MEXPOST, which takes 10–15 days for delivery. International mail companies are recommended for urgent mailings.

▼ Food

Eating Out

Essential

Can you recommend a good *restaurant/ bar*?	**¿Puede recomendarme un buen *restaurante/bar*?** pweh•deh rreh•koh•mehn•dahr•meh oon bwehn *rrehs•taw•rahn•teh/bahr*
Is there *a traditional/ an inexpensive* restaurant nearby?	**¿Hay un restaurante *típico/barato* cerca de aquí?** aye oon rrehs•taw•rahn•teh *tee•pee•koh/bah•rah•toh* sehr•kah deh ah•kee
A table for…, please.	**Una mesa para…, por favor.** oo•nah meh•sah pah•rah…pohr fah•bohr
Can we sit…?	**¿Podemos sentarnos…?** poh•deh•mohs sehn•tahr•nohs…
– here/there	**– aquí/allá** ah•kee/ah•yah
– outside	**– afuera** ah•fweh•rah
– in a non-smoking area	**– en el área de no fumar** ehn ehl ah•reh•ah deh noh foo•mahr
I'm waiting for someone.	**Estoy esperando a alguien.** ehs•toy ehs•peh•rahn•doh ah ahl•geeyehn
Where's the restroom [toilet]?	**¿Dónde está el baño?** dohn•deh ehs•tah ehl bah•nyo
A menu, please.	**Un menú, por favor.** oon meh•noo pohr fah•bohr
What do you recommend?	**¿Qué me recomienda?** keh meh rreh•koh•meeyehn•dah
I'd like…	**Quiero…** keeyeh•roh…
Some more…, please.	**Quiero más…, por favor.** keeyeh•roh mahs…pohr fah•bohr

Enjoy your meal! **¡Buen provecho!** bwen proh·beh·choh

The check [bill], please. **La cuenta, por favor.** lah kwen·tah pohr fah·bohr

Is service included? **¿Está incluido el cubierto?** ehs·tah een·kloo·ee·doh ehl koo·beeyehr·toh

Can I pay by credit card? **¿Puedo pagar con tarjeta de crédito?** pweh·doh pah·gahr kohn tahr·kheh·tah deh kreh·dee·toh

Can I have a receipt? **¿Podría darme un comprobante?** poh·dree·ah dahr·meh oon kohm·proh·bahn·teh

Thank you! **¡Gracias!** grah·seeyahs

Restaurant Types

Can you recommend...? **¿Puede recomendarme...?** pweh·deh rreh·koh·mehn·dahr·meh...

– a bar **– un bar** oon bahr

– a cafe **– un café** oon kah·feh

– a fast-food place **– un restaurante de comida rápida** oon rrehs·taw·rahn·teh deh koh·mee·dah rrah·pee·dah

– a restaurant **– un restaurante** oon rrehs·taw·rahn·teh

Reservations and Questions

I'd like to reserve a table... **Quiero reservar una mesa...** keeyeh·roh rreh·sehr·bahr oo·nah meh·sah ...

– for 2 **– para dos** pah·rah dohs

– for this evening **– para esta noche** pah·rah ehs·tah noh·cheh

– for tomorrow at... **– para mañana a la/las...** pah·rah mah·nyah·nah ah lah/lahs...

▶For when to use **la** or **las**, see page 174.

A table for 2, please.	**Una mesa para dos, por favor.** oo•nah meh•sah pah•rah dohs pohr fah•bohr
We have a reservation.	**Tenemos una reserva.** teh•neh•mohs oo•nah rreh•sehr•bah
My name is…	**Me llamo…** meh yah•moh…
Can we sit…?	**¿Podríamos sentarnos…?** poh•dree•ah•mohs sehn•tahr•nohs…
– here/there	**– aquí/allá** ah•kee/ah•ya
– outside	**– afuera** ah•fweh•rah
– in a non-smoking area	**– en el área de no fumar** ehn ehl ah•reh•ah deh noh foo•mahr
– by the window	**– junto a la ventana** khoon•toh ah lah behn•tah•nah
Where's the restroom [toilet]?	**¿Dónde está el baño?** dohn•deh ehs•tah ehl bah•nyoh

You May Hear...

¿Tiene reserva? teeyeh•neh rreh•sehr•bah	Do you have a reservation?
¿Cuántos son? kwahn•tohs sohn	How many?
¿En el área de fumar o no fumar? ehn ehl ah•reh•ah deh foo•mahr oh noh foo•mahr	Smoking or non-smoking?
¿Está listo♂/lista♀ para pedir? ehs•tah lees•toh♂/lees•tah♀ pah•rah peh•deer	Are you ready to order?
¿Qué va a ordenar? keh bah ah orh•deh•nahr	What would you like?
Le recomiendo... leh reh•koh•meeyehn•doh...	I recommend...
Buen provecho. bwen proh•beh•choh	Enjoy your meal.

Ordering

Waiter/Waitress!	**¡Mesero♂/Mesera♀!** meh•seh•roh♂/meh•seh•rah♀
We're ready to order.	**Estamos listos para pedir.** ehs•tah•mohs lees•tohs pah•rah peh•deer
The wine list, please.	**La carta de vinos, por favor.** lah kahr•tah deh bee•nohs pohr fah•bohr
I'd like...	**Quiero...** keeyeh•roh...
– a bottle of...	**– una botella de...** oo•nah boh•teh•yah deh...
– a carafe of...	**– una jarra de...** oo•nah khahr•rrah deh...
– a glass of...	**– un vaso de...** oon bah•soh deh...
The menu, please.	**La carta, por favor.** lah kahr•tah pohr fah•bohr

▶For alcoholic and non-alcoholic drinks, see page 86.

Do you have...?	**¿Tiene...?** teeyeh•neh...
– a children's menu	**– un menú para niños** oon meh•noo pah•rah nee•nyohs
– a fixed-price menu	**– el menú del día** ehl meh•noo dehl dee•ah
– a menu in English	**– un menú en inglés** oon meh•noo ehn een•glehs
What do you recommend?	**¿Qué me recomienda?** keh meh rreh•koh•meeyehn•dah
What's this?	**¿Qué es esto?** keh ehs ehs•toh
What's in it?	**¿Qué lleva?** keh yeh•bah
Is it spicy?	**¿Es picante?** ehs pee•kahn•teh
Without..., please.	**Sin..., por favor.** seen...pohr fah•bohr
It's to go [take away].	**Es para llevar.** ehs pah•rah yeh•bahr

You May See...

CARTA	menu
MENÚ DEL DÍA	menu of the day
CUBIERTO (NO) INCLUIDO	service (not) included
ESPECIALIDADES DE LA CASA	specials

Cooking Methods

baked	**al horno** ah ohr•noh
boiled	**hervido** ♂ **/hervida** ♀ ehr•bee•doh ♂ ehr•bee•dah ♀
braised	**a fuego lento** ah fweh•goh lehn•toh

breaded	**empanizado♂/empanizada♀** ehm•pah•nee•sah•doh♂/ehm•pah•nee•sah•dah♀
creamed	**con crema** kohn kreh•mah
diced	**cortado en cuadritos** kohr•tah•doh ehn kwah•dree•tohs
fileted	**fileteado** fee•leh•teh•ah•doh
fried	**frito♂/frita♀** free•toh♂/free•tah♀
grilled	**a la plancha** ah lah plahn•chah
poached	**escalfado♂/escalfada♀** ehs•kahl•fah•doh♂/ ehs•kahl•fah•dah♀
roasted	**asado♂/asada♀** ah•sah•doh♂/ah•sah•dah♀
sautéed	**salteado♂/salteada♀** sahl•teh•ah•doh♂/ sahl•teh•ah•dah♀
smoked	**ahumado♂/ahumada♀** ah•oo•mah•doh♂/ ah•oo•mah•dah♀
steamed	**al vapor** ahl bah•pohr
stewed	**guisado♂/guisada♀** gee•sah•doh♂/ gee•sah•dah♀
stuffed	**relleno♂/rellena♀** rreh•yeh•noh♂/ rreh•yeh•nah♀

Special Requirements

I'm...	**Soy...** soy...
– diabetic	**– diabético♂/diabética♀** deeyah•beh•tee•koh♂/deeyah•beh•tee•kah♀
– lactose intolerant	**– intolerante a la lactosa** een•toh•leh•rahn•teh ah lah lahk•toh•sah
– vegetarian	**– vegetariano♂/vegetariana♀** beh•kheh•tah•reeyah•noh♂/ beh•kheh•tah•reeyah•nah♀

I'm allergic to…	**Soy alérgico♂/alérgica♀ a…** soy ah•lehr•khee•koh♂/ah•lehr•khee•kah♀ ah…
I can't eat…	**No puedo comer…** noh pweh•doh koh•mehr…
– dairy	**– productos lácteos** proh•dook•tohs lahk•teh•ohs
– gluten	**– gluten** gloo•tehn
– nuts	**– frutos secos** froo•tohs seh•kohs
– pork	**– carne de puerco** kahr•neh deh pwehr•koh
– shellfish	**– mariscos** mah•rees•kohs
– spicy foods	**– comidas picantes** koh•mee•dahs pee•kahn•tehs
– wheat	**– trigo** tree•goh
Is it *halal/kosher*?	**¿Es *halal/kosher*?** ehs *ah•lahl/koh•shehr*

Dining with Kids

Do you have children's portions?	**¿Sirven raciones para niños?** seer•behn rrah•seeyoh•nehs pah•rah nee•nyohs
A *highchair/child's seat*, please.	**Una *periquera/silla para niños*, por favor.** oo•nah *peh•ree•keh•rah/see•yah pah•rah nee•nyohs* pohr fah•bohr
Where can I *feed/change* the baby?	**¿Dónde puedo *darle de comer/cambiar* al niño?** dohn•deh pweh•doh *dahr•leh deh koh•mehr/kahm•beeyahr* ahl nee•nyoh
Can you warm this?	**¿Puede calentar esto?** pweh•deh kah•lehn•tahr ehs•toh

▶For travel with children, see page 155.

Complaints

How much longer will our food be?	**¿Cuánto más tardará la comida?** kwahn•toh mahs tahr•dah•rah lah koh•mee•dah

We can't wait any longer.	**No podemos esperar más.** noh poh•deh•mohs ehs•peh•rahr mahs
We're leaving.	**Nos vamos.** nohs bah•mohs
I didn't order this.	**Esto no es lo que pedí.** ehs•toh noh ehs loh keh peh•dee
I ordered…	**Pedí…** peh•dee…
I can't eat this.	**No puedo comerme esto.** noh pweh•doh koh•mehr•meh ehs•toh
This is too…	**Esto está demasiado…** ehs•toh ehs•tah deh•mah•seeyah•doh…
– cold/hot	**– frío/caliente** free•oh/kah•leeyehn•teh
– salty/spicy	**– salado/picante** sah•lah•doh/pee•kahn•teh
– tough/bland	**– duro/insípido** doo•roh/een•see•pee•doh
This isn't *clean/fresh*.	**Esto no está *limpio/fresco*.** ehs•toh noh ehs•tah *leem•peeyoh/frehs•koh*

Paying

The check [bill], please.	**La cuenta, por favor.** lah kwehn•tah pohr fah•bohr
Separate checks [bills], please.	**Cuentas separadas, por favor.** kwehn•tahs seh•pah•rah•dahs pohr fah•bohr
It's all together.	**Póngalo todo junto.** pohn•gah•loh toh•doh khoon•toh
Is service included?	**¿Está incluido el cubierto?** ehs•tah een•kloo•ee•doh ehl koo•beeyehr•toh
What's this amount for?	**¿De qué es esta cantidad?** deh keh ehs ehs•tah kahn•tee•dahd
I didn't have that. I had…	**Yo no ordené eso. Tomé…** yoh noh ohr•deh•neh eh•soh toh•meh…
Can I pay by credit card?	**¿Aceptan tarjeta de crédito?** ah•sehp•tahn tahr•kheh•tah deh kreh•dee•toh

Can I have *a receipt/ an itemized bill*?	**¿Podría darme *un comprobante/una cuenta detallada*?** poh·dree·ah dahr·meh *oon kohm·proh·bahn·teh/oo·nah kwehn·tah deh·tah·yah·dah*
That was delicious!	**¡Estuvo delicioso!** ehs·too·boh deh·lee·seeyoh·soh

Although restaurants are generally required to include a service charge as part of the bill (you will see this charge as **cubierto**), a tip of 10–15% is also customary.

Market

Where are the *carts [trolleys]/baskets*?	**¿Dónde están *los carritos/las canastas*?** dohn·deh ehs·tahn *lohs kah·rree·tohs/lahs kah·nahs·tahs*
Where is...?	**¿Donde está...?** dohn·deh ehs·tah...

►For food items, see page 90.

I'd like some of *that/this.*	**Quiero un poco de *eso/esto*.** keeyeh·roh oon poh·koh deh *eh·soh/ehs·toh*
Can I taste it?	**¿Puedo probarlo?** pweh·doh proh·bahr·loh
I'd like...	**Quiero...** keeyeh·roh...
– a *kilo/half-kilo* of...	**– un *kilo/medio kilo* de...** oon *kee·loh/ meh·deeyoh kee·loh* deh...
– a liter of...	**– un litro de...** oon lee·troh deh...
– a piece of...	**– un trozo de...** oon troh·soh deh...
– a slice of...	**– una rebanada de...** oo·nah reh·bah·nah·dah deh...
More./Less.	**Más./Menos.** mahs/meh·nohs
How much?	**¿Cuánto es?** kwahn·toh ehs
Where do I pay?	**¿Dónde pago?** dohn·deh pah·goh

A bag, please.	**Una bolsa, por favor.** oo·nah bohl·sah pohr fah·bohr
I'm being helped.	**Ya me están atendiendo.** yah meh ehs·tahn ah·tehn·deeyehn·doh

▶For conversion tables, see page 183.

You May Hear...

¿Necesita ayuda? neh·seh·see·tah ah·yoo·dah	Can I help you?
¿Qué desea? keh deh·seh·ah	What would you like?
¿Algo más? ahl·goh mahs	Anything else?
Son...pesos. sohn...peh·sohs	That's...pesos.

In Mexico, food is often purchased at local family-run markets or farmer's markets. These are excellent places for regional and specialty food such as fresh fruit and vegetables, meat and baked goods.

Supermercados (supermarkets) are also common, but these are usually found only in big cities. These stores have a larger selection than regular markets, and can be less expensive.

You May See...

CONSUMIR PREFERENTEMENTE ANTES DE...	best if used by...
CALORÍAS	calories
SIN GRASA	fat free
CONSERVAR EN REFRIGERACIÓN	keep refrigerated

PUEDE CONTENER RASTROS DE...	may contain traces of...
VENDER HASTA...	sell by...
APTO PARA VEGETARIANOS	suitable for vegetarians

Dishes, Utensils and Kitchen Tools

bottle opener	**el destapador** ehl dehs•tah•pah•dohr
bowl	**el tazón** ehl tah•sohn
can opener	**el abrelatas** ehl ah•breh•lah•tahs
corkscrew	**el sacacorchos** ehl sah•kah•kohr•chohs
cup	**la taza** lah tah•sah
fork	**el tenedor** ehl teh•neh•dohr
frying pan	**el sartén** ehl sahr•tehn
glass	**el vaso** ehl bah•soh
(steak) knife	**el cuchillo (de carne)** ehl koo•chee•yoh (deh kahr•neh)
napkin	**la servilleta** lah sehr•bee•yeh•tah
plate	**el plato** ehl plah•toh
pot	**la olla** lah oh•yah
pottery saucepan	**la cazuela de barro** lah kah•sweh•lah deh bah•rroh
saucepan	**la cacerola** lah kah•seh•roh•lah
spatula	**la espátula** lah ehs•pah•too•lah
spoon	**la cuchara** lah koo•chah•rah
stone bowl for salsa	**el molcajete** ehl mohl•kah•kheh•teh
tortilla maker	**la tortilladora** lah tohr•tee•yah•doh•rah

Meals

El desayuno (breakfast) is usually served from 7:00 a.m. to 10:00 a.m. **La comida** (lunch), generally the largest meal of the day, is served from 1:00 p.m. to 4:00 p.m. **La cena** (dinner) is typically smaller and lighter than in the U.S. or U.K., and is usually served after 8:00 p.m.

Breakfast

el agua ehl ah·gwah	water
la avena lah ah·beh·nah	oatmeal
el café/el té… ehl kah·feh/ehl teh…	coffee/tea…
– con azúcar kohn ah·soo·kahr	– with sugar
– descafeinado dehs·kah·feh·ee·nah·doh	– decaf
– con endulzante artificial kohn ehn·dool·sahn·teh ahr·tee·fee·seeyahl	– with artificial sweetener
– con leche kohn leh·cheh	– with milk
– solo soh·loh	– black
las carnes frías lahs kahr·nehs free·ahs	cold cuts [charcuterie]
los cereales (calientes/fríos) lohs seh·reh·ah·lehs (kah·leeyehn·tehs/free·ohs)	(cold/hot) cereal
las frutas lahs froo·tahs	fruit
el huevo… ehl weh·boh…	egg…
– duro/tibio doo·roh/tee·beeyoh	– *hard-/soft*-boiled
– frito free·toh	– fried
– revuelto rreh·bwehl·toh	– scrambled

I'd like…	**Quiero…** keeyeh·roh…
More…, please.	**Más…, por favor.** mahs…pohr fah·bohr

el jugo ehl khoo•goh	juice
la leche lah leh•cheh	milk
la mantequilla lah mahn•teh•kee•yah	butter
la mermelada/la jalea lah mehr•meh•lah•dah/khah•leh•ah	jam/jelly
el omelet… ehl oh•meh•leht…	omelet…
– con champiñones kohn chahm•pee•nyoh•nehs	– with mushrooms
– con jamón kohn khah•mohn	– with ham
– con queso kohn keh•soh	– with cheese
el pan ehl pahn	bread
el pan tostado ehl pahn tohs•tah•doh	toast
el queso ehl keh•soh	cheese
la salchicha lah sahl•chee•chah	sausage
el sándwich… ehl sahnd•weech…	sandwich…
– de huevo deh weh•boh	– with egg
– de jamón y queso deh kha•mohn ee keh•soh	– with ham and cheese
– de pollo deh poh•yoh	– with chicken
el yogur ehl yoh•goor	yogurt

Appetizers [Starters]

las chalupas lahs chah•loo•pahs	tortillas with potato, chicken, onion and salsa topping
el chicharrón ehl chee•chah•rrohn	deep fried pork skin
los frijoles refritos lohs free•khoh•lehs rreh•free•tohs	mashed and fried black beans

With/Without…	**Con/Sin…** kohn/seen…
I can't have…	**No puedo comer…** noh pweh•doh koh•mehr…

las gorditas lahs gohr•dee•tahs	little corn cakes baked or fried
el guacamole ehl gwa•hkah•moh•leh	mashed avocado, onions, tomatoes and lime juice
las quesadillas lahs keh•sah•dee•yahs	corn tortillas stuffed with cheese, beef, chicken, etc.
el queso fundido ehl keh•soh foon•dee•doh	Mexican fondue
la salsa lah sahl•sah	chopped or pureed tomatoes, chiles, onions and cilantro
los tacos lohs tah•kohs	soft tortillas filled with a variety of meat and vegetables
la tortilla lah tohr•tee•yah	thin, flat bread made of corn

Botanas are snacks, similar to appetizers, served in cafes, bars and restaurants. Many bars (also known as **cantinas**) and restaurants have their own specialties.

You may have already sampled **tacos**, but note that authentic Mexican **tacos** are made with a soft, not fried, **tortilla.** For deep fried tacos, try **tacos dorados.** Other taco specialties include **tacos de cazuela,** made with various regional fillings simmered in large earthenware pots, and the famous **tacos al pastor** with marinated pork and/or beef cooked on a rotisserie with pineapple on top.

I'd like…	**Quiero…** keeyeh•roh…
More…, please.	**Más…, por favor.** mahs…pohr fah•bohr

Soup

caldo tlalpeño kahl•doh tlahl•peh•nyo	soup made with vegetables, chicken and sometimes rice
crema creh•mah	soup made with cream and assorted ingredients
pozole poh•soh•leh	soup of stewed pork and corn kernels, garnished with lettuce, horseradish and oregano
sopa de lima soh•pah deh lee•mah	lima (citrus fruit) soup with seasoned chicken broth
sopa de tortilla soh•pah deh tohr•tee•yah	tomato broth garnished with fried tortilla strips, cream, avocado, cheese, chile and pork skin

With/Without...	**Con/Sin...** kohn/seen...
I can't have...	**No puedo comer...** noh pweh•doh koh•mehr...

Fish and Seafood

la almeja lah ahl•meh•khah	clam
la anchoa lah ahn•choh•ah	fresh baby anchovy
los anillos de calamar lohs ah•nee•yohs deh kah•lah•mahr	deep-fried squid
el arenque ehl ah•rehn•keh	herring
el atún ehl ah•toon	tuna
el bacalao ehl bah•kah•la•oh	cod
el besugo ehl beh•soo•goh	sea bream
los callos de hacha lohs kah•yohs deh ah•chah	scallops
el cangrejo ehl kahn•greh•khoh	crab
el cazón ehl kah•sohn	baby shark
las cigalas lahs see•gah•lahs	crayfish
los langostinos lohs lahn•gohs•tee•nohs	prawn
la langosta lah lahn•gohs•tah	lobster
el lenguado ehl lehn•gwah•doh	sole
la lubina lah loo•bee•nah	sea bass
los mejillones lohs meh•khee•yoh•nehs	mussels
los mejillones en escabeche lohs meh•khee•yohn•ehs ehn ehs•kah•beh•cheh	mussels in a marinade
la merluza lah mehr•loo•sah	hake
el mero ehl meh•roh	grouper
la mojarra lah moh•khah•rrah	mackerel
la ostra lah ohs•trah	oyster

I'd like…	**Quiero…** keeyeh•roh…
More…, please.	**Más…, por favor.** mahs…pohr fah•vohr

el pampanito ehl pahm•pah•nee•toh	yellowtail
el pez espada ehl pehs ehs•pah•dah	swordfish
el pulpo ehl pool•poh	octopus
el pulpo al olivo ehl pool•poh ahl oh•lee•boh	octopus with olive
el salmón ehl sahl•mohn	salmon
el tiburón ehl tee•boo•rohn	shark
la tilapia lah tee•lah•peeyah	tilapia
la trucha lah troo•chah	trout
la trucha ahumada lah troo•chah aw•mah•dah	smoked trout

Ceviche

ceviche... seh•bee•cheh...	marinated, raw...
– de callos de hacha deh kah•yohs deh ah•chah	– scallops
– de camarones deh kah•mah•roh•nehs	– shrimp
– de langostinos deh lahn•gohs•tee•nohs	– prawn
– de mariscos deh mah•rees•kohs	– mixed seafood
– de pescado deh pehs•kah•do	– fish
– de pulpo deh pool•poh	– octopus

Ceviche is made by marinating raw fish with lime. The citrus adds flavor and "cooks" the fish without heat. The preparation includes chopped onions, tomato and olives, with a dash of hot **salsa**. **Ceviche** is served cold accompanied with crackers.

With/Without...	**Con/Sin...** kohn/seen...
I can't have...	**No puedo tomar...** noh pweh•doh toh•mahr...

Meat and Poultry

el bife angosto	ehl bee•feh ahn•gohs•toh	strip steak
el bistec	ehl bees•tehk	beefsteak
el cabrito	ehl kah•bree•toh	roast kid (young goat)
la carne	lah kahr•neh	meat
la carne de asada	lah kahr•neh ah•sah•dah	grilled meat
la carne de puerco	lah kahr•neh deh pwehr•koh	pork
la carne de res	lah kahr•neh deh rehs	beef
la carne molida	lah kahr•neh moh•lee•dah	ground beef
el chorizo	ehl choh•ree•soh	highly-seasoned pork sausage
la chuleta	lah choo•leh•tah	chop
la codorniz	lah koh•dohr•nees	quail
el conejo	ehl koh•neh•khoh	rabbit
el cordero	ehl kohr•deh•roh	lamb
las costillas de puerco	lahs kohs•tee•yahs deh pwehr•koh	pork ribs
la falda	lah fahl•dah	beef flank steak
el filete	ehl fee•leh•teh	steak
el hígado…	ehl ee•gah•doh…	…liver
– de cordero	deh kohr•deh•roh	– lamb
– de pollo	deh poh•yoh	– chicken
– de res	deh rrehs	– beef
el jamón	ehl khah•mohn	ham

I'd like…	**Quiero…** keeyeh•roh…
More…, please.	**Más…, por favor.** mahs…pohr fah•bohr

el jamón serrano ehl khah•mohn seh•rrah•noh — dry-cured serrano ham

el lomo ehl loh•moh — loin

las mollejas de ternera lahs moh•yeh•khahs deh tehr•neh•rah — veal sweetbread

la moronga lah moh•rohn•gah — blood sausage

las patas de puerco lahs pah•tahs deh pwehr•koh — pig's feet [trotters]

el pato ehl pah•toh — duck

el pavo ehl pah•boh — turkey

el pollo ehl poh•yoh — chicken

el pollo frito ehl poh•yoh free•toh — fried chicken

el riñón ehl rree•nyohn — kidney

la riñonada lah rree•nyo•nah•dah — kidney stew

la salchicha lah sahl•chee•chah — sausage

el salchichón ehl sahl•chee•chohn — salami-type sausage

el sirloin ehl seer•loh•een — sirloin

la ternera lah tehr•neh•rah — veal

el tocino ehl toh•see•noh — bacon

el venado ehl beh•nah•doh — venison

rare	**de vuelta y vuelta** deh bwehl•tah ee bwehl•tah
medium	**término medio** tehr•meeh•noh meh•deeyoh
well-done	**bien cocido♂/cocida♀** beeyehn koh•sih•doh♂/ koh•sih•dah♀

With/Without…	**Con/Sin…** kohn/seen…
I can't have…	**No puedo tomar…** noh pweh•doh toh•mahr…

Meat dishes are popular in Mexico, and the northern states of Sonora and Chihuahua are famous for their cuts of beef. Traditional dishes include **carne asada** (grilled meat), which is usually served with a side of **tortillas**, beans, grilled onions and **salsa**. Another Mexican specialty is the **barbacoa**: mutton cooked in the ground with spices and wrapped in **maguey** leaves. The resulting broth is seasoned and served as a soup.

The **torta,** which is basically a sandwich made with a kind of white bread, is also a specialty. These are filled with **frijoles refritos** (mashed and fried black beans), meat, lettuce, tomato, onion and chile, among other things. They can have many ingredients or just a few, depending on each person's taste.

Vegetables

la aceituna lah ah•seyee•too•nah	olive
la acelga lah ah•sehl•gah	chard
el aguacate ehl ah•gwah•khah•teh	avocado
el ajo ehl ah•khoh	garlic
la alcachofa lah ahl•kah•choh•fah	artichoke
el apio ehl ah•peeyoh	celery
la berenjena lah beh•rehn•kheh•nah	eggplant [aubergine]
el brócoli ehl broh•koh•lee	broccoli
el calabacita lah kah•lah•bah•see•tah	zucchini [courgette]
el camote ehl kah•moh•teh	yam
la cebolla lah seh•boh•yah	onion

I'd like…	**Quiero…** keeyeh•roh…
More…, please.	**Más…, por favor.** mahs…pohr fah•bohr

el champiñón (a la plancha/salteado) ehl chahm•pee•nyohn (ah lah plahn•chah/sahl•teh•ah•doh)	(grilled/sautéed) mushroom
el chícharo ehl chee•chah•roh	green pea
el chile ehl chee•leh	hot pepper
el chile chipotle ehl chee•leh chee•poh•tleh	chipotle pepper
el chile jalapeño ehl chee•leh khah•lah•peh•nyo	jalapeño pepper
el chile verde ehl chee•leh behr•deh	hot green pepper
la col lah kohl	cabbage
la coliflor lah koh•lee•flohr	cauliflower
el ejote ehl eh•khoh•teh	green bean
el espárrago ehl ehs•pah•rrah•goh	asparagus
la espinaca lah ehs•pee•nah•kah	spinach
los frijoles lah free•kho•lehs	beans
el germinado de soya ehl gehr•mee•nah•doh deh soh•yah	bean sprouts
las habas lahs ah•bahs	broad beans
el jitomate ehl khee•toh•mah•teh	tomato
la lechuga lah leh•choo•gah	lettuce
la lenteja lah lehn•teh•khah	lentil
el maíz ehl mah•ees	corn
la papa lah pah•pah	potato
el pepino ehl peh•pee•noh	cucumber

With/Without…	**Con/Sin…** kohn/seen…
I can't have…	**No puedo comer…** noh pweh•doh koh•mehr…

el pimiento *rojo/verde* ehl pee•meeyehn•toh *roh•khoh/behr•deh*	*red/green* pepper
la verdura lah behr•doo•rah	vegetable
la zanahoria lah sah•nah•oh•reeyah	carrot

Spices and Staples

la albahaca lah ahl•bah•kah	basil
la alcaparra lah ahl•kah•pah•rrah	caper
la almendra lah ahl•mehn•drah	almond
el anís ehl ah•nees	aniseed
el arroz… ehl ah•rrohs…	rice…
– a la jardinera ah lah khar•dee•neh•rah	– with corn and peas
– a la mexicana ah lah meh•khee•kah•nah	– with tomatoes and seasoning
– blanco blahn•koh	– white
– con frijoles kohn free•khoh•les	– with beans
– con mariscos kohn mah•rees•kohs	– with seafood
– con pollo kohn poh•yoh	– with chicken
– rojo rroh•khoh	– red
el azafrán ehl ah•sah•frahn	saffron
el azúcar ehl ah•soo•kahr	sugar
la harina lah ah•ree•nah	flour
la mantequilla (*con/sin* sal) lah mahn•teh•kee•yah (*kohn/seen* sahl)	butter (*with/without* salt)
la margarina lah mahr•gah•ree•nah	margarine

I'd like…	**Quiero…** keeyeh•roh…
More…, please.	**Más…, por favor.** mahs…pohr fah•bohr

el pan ehl pahn	bread
la pasta lah pahs•tah	pasta
el perejil ehl peh•reh•kheel	parsley
la pimienta negra lah pee•meeyehn•tah neh•grah	black pepper
la sal lah sahl	salt
la tortilla lah tohr•tee•yah	tortilla

Fruit

el arándano ehl ah•rahn•dah•noh	blueberry
el arándano rojo ehl ah•rahn•dah•noh roh•khoh	cranberry
la cereza lah seh•reh•sah	cherry
el chabacano ehl chah•bah•kah•noh	apricot
la chirimoya lah chee•ree•moh•yah	custard apple
la ciruela lah see•rweh•lah	plum
el coco ehl koh•koh	coconut
el durazno ehl duh•rahs•noh	peach
la frambuesa lah frahm•bweh•sah	raspberry
la fresa lah freh•sah	strawberry
la fruta lah froo•tah	fruit
la granada roja lah grah•nah•dah roh•khah	pomegranate
la guayaba lah gwah•yah•bah	guava
el kiwi ehl kee•wee	kiwi
el limón ehl lee•mohn	lime
el limón amarillo ehl lee•mohn ah•mah•ree•yoh	lemon

With/Without...	**Con/Sin...** kohn/seen...
I can't have...	**No puedo comer...** noh pweh•doh koh•mehr...

el mamey ehl mah•mehy — mamey (type of tropical fruit)

el mango ehl mahn•goh — mango

la mandarina lah mahn•dah•ree•nah — tangerine

la manzana lah mahn•sah•nah — apple

el maracuyá ehl mah•rah•coo•yah — passion fruit

el melón ehl meh•lohn — melon

la naranja lah nah•rahn•khah — orange

la nectarina lah nehk•tah•ree•nah — nectarine

la papaya lah pah•pah•yah — papaya

la pera lah peh•rah — pear

la piña lah pee•nyah — pineapple

el plátano ehl plah•tah•noh — banana

la sandía lah sahn•dee•ah — watermelon

el tamarindo ehl tah•mah•reen•doh — tamarind

la toronja lah toh•rohn•khah — grapefruit

la uva lah oo•bah — grape

Cheese

el queso… ehl keh•soh… — …cheese

– añejo ah•nyeh•khoh — – ripe

– asadero ah•sah•deh•roh — – mild-flavored, essential for making quesadillas

– chihuahua chee•wah•wah — – yellow

– cremoso kreh•moh•soh — – cream

I'd like…	**Quiero…** keeyeh•roh…
More…, please.	**Más…, por favor.** mahs…pohr fah•bohr

– **de leche de cabra** deh leh•cheh deh kah•brah	– goat's milk
– **duro** doo•roh	– hard
– **fuerte** fwehr•teh	– strong
– **jalapeño** khah•lah•peh•nyo	– jalapeño pepper
– **oaxaca** oh•ah•khah•kah	– similar to mozzarella
– **panela** pah•neh•lah	– white
– **parmesano** pahr•meh•sah•noh	– parmesan
– **rallado** rrah•yah•doh	– grated
– **requesón** rreh•keh•sohn	– similar to ricotta

Dessert

el arroz con leche ehl ah•rrohs kohn leh•cheh	rice pudding
el ate ehl ah•teh	fruit and sugar dessert
el brazo de gitano ehl brah•soh deh khee•tah•noh	sponge cake roll with cream filling
el buñuelo ehl boo•nyweh•loh	thin, deep-fried fritter, covered in sugar
la cajeta lah kah•kheh•tah	cooked goat's milk with sugar
el churro ehl choo•rroh	deep-fried fritter sprinkled with sugar
la crepa lah kreh•pah	crepe (used in sweet or savory dishes)
el flan ehl flahn	caramel custard
la galleta lah gah•yeh•tah	cookie [biscuit]

With/Without...	**Con/Sin...** kohn/seen...
I can't have...	**No puedo tomar...** noh pweh•doh toh•mahr...

la gelatina lah kheh•lah•tee•nah	gelatin dessert
el helado ehl eh•lah•doh	ice cream
la leche frita lah leh•cheh free•tah	fried milk custard
la mantecada lah mahn•teh•kah•dah	small sponge cake
la manzana horneada lah mahn•sah•nah ohr•neh•ah•dah	baked apple
la nieve lah nyeh•beh	sorbet
la palanqueta lah pah•lahn•keh•tah	kind of peanut butter
el pastel de manzana ehl pahs•tehl deh mahn•sah•nah	apple pie
el pie de limón ehl pahee deh lee•mohn	key lime pie
el pie de queso ehl pahee deh keh•soh	cheesecake

One of Mexico's most widely enjoyed culinary exports is **chocolate** (chocolate). Chocolate is made from cacao, and has been enjoyed in various forms for the last three thousand years. You'll find that Mexican chocolate is usually dark and is combined with sugar, cinnamon and often nuts.

Another specialty is **cajeta**, caramelized cow's or goat's milk. It is a traditional Mexican sweet that may be enjoyed on its own or as a topping for pastries, bread and even ice cream.

Drinks

Essential

The *wine list/drink menu*, please. **La carta de *vinos/bebidas*, por favor.** lah kahr·tah deh *bee·nohs/beh·bee·dahs* pohr fah·bohr

What do you recommend? **¿Qué me recomienda?** keh meh rreh·koh·meeyehn·dah

I'd like a *bottle/glass* of *red/white* wine. **Quiero *una botella/una copa* de vino *tinto/blanco.*** keeyeh·roh *oo·nah boh·teh·yah/oo·nah koh·pah* deh bee·noh *teen·toh/blahn·koh*

The house wine, please. **El vino de la casa, por favor.** ehl bee·noh deh lah kah·sah pohr fah·bohr

Another *bottle/glass*, please. **Otra *botella/copa*, por favor.** oh·trah *boh·teh·yah/koh·pah* pohr fah·bohr

I'd like a local beer. **Quiero una cerveza nacional.** keeyeh·roh oo·nah sehr·beh·sah nah·seeoh·nhal

Can I buy you a drink? **¿Puedo invitarle una copa?** pweh·doh een·bee·tahr·leh oo·nah koh·pah

Cheers! **¡Salud!** sah·lood

A *coffee/tea*, please. **Un *café/té*, por favor.** oon *kah·feh/teh* pohr fah·bohr

Black. **Solo.** soh·loh

With… **Con…** kohn…

– artificial sweetener **– endulzante artificial** ehn·dool·sahn·teh ahr·tee·fee·seeyahl

– milk **– leche** leh·cheh

– sugar **– azúcar** ah·soo·kahr

..., please.	**..., por favor.** ...pohr fah·boh
– A juice	**– Un jugo** khoo·goh
– A soda	**– Un refresco** rreh·frehs·koh
– A (sparkling/still) water	**– Un agua (*con/sin* gas)** ah·gwah (*kohn/ seen* gahs)
Is the tap water safe to drink?	**¿Se puede beber el agua de la llave?** seh pweh·deh beh·behr ehl ah·gwah deh lah yah·beh

Non-alcoholic Drinks

el agua (*con/sin* gas) ehl ah·gwah (*kohn/seen* gahs)	(sparkling/still) water
el atole ehl ah·toh·leh	a hot drink made from corn
el café ehl kah·feh	coffee
el chocolate caliente ehl choh·koh·lah·teh kah·leeyehn·teh	hot chocolate
el jugo de... ehl khoo·goh deh...	...juice
– manzana mahn·sah·nah	– apple
– naranja nah·rahn·khah	– orange
– toronja toh·rohn·khah	– grapefruit
la leche lah leh·cheh	milk
la limonada lah lee·moh·nah·dah	lemonade
la naranjada lah nah·rahn·khah·dah	orange soft drink
el raspado ehl rrahs·pah·doh	sorbet
el refresco ehl rreh·frehs·koh	soda
el té helado ehl teh eh·lah·doh	iced tea

Many Mexicans love coffee and drink it throughout the day. **Café de olla** is coffee prepared in a clay pot, sweetened with **piloncillo** (brown sugar). **Café lechero** is coffee mixed with steamed milk.

Tap water is not always safe to drink for foreigners. Restaurants often serve bottled water with meals, unless you specifically request **agua de la llave** (tap water). Juice is usually served with breakfast, but it's not common at lunch or dinner.

Aperitifs, Cocktails and Liqueurs

el coñac ehl koh•nyahk — cognac

la ginebra lah khee•neh•brah — gin

el jerez fino ehl kheh•rehs fee•noh — pale, dry sherry

el jerez oscuro ehl kheh•rehs ohs•koo•roh — dark, heavy sherry

el licor ehl lee•kohr — liqueur

el oporto ehl oh•pohr•toh — port

el ron ehl rrohn — rum

la sangría lah sahn·gree·ah — wine punch

el tequila ehl teh·kee·lah — tequila

el vodka ehl bohd·kah — vodka

el whisky ehl wees·kee — whisky

Beer

la cerveza... lah sehr·beh·sah... — ...beer

– **en botella/de barril** ehn boh·teh·yah/deh bah·rreel — – bottled/draft

– **nacional/importada** nah·seeyoh·nahl/ eem·pohr·tah·dah — – local/imported

– **oscura/clara** ohs·koo·rah/klah·rah — – dark/light

– **rubia** roo·beeyah — – lager

– **sin alcohol** seen ahl·koh·ohl — – non-alcoholic

There are many popular brands of Mexican beer, such as **Corona®**, **Sol®**, **Tecate®** and **Victoria®**, to name a few. Each brand usually has several classes and types of beer available, though most will be a lager-type beer.

You May Hear...

¿Qué desea tomar? keh deh•seh•ah toh•mahr	What would you like to drink?
¿Con leche o azúcar? kohn leh•cheh oh ah•soo•kahr	With milk or sugar?
¿Agua con gas o sin gas? ah•gwah kohn gahs oh seen gahs	Sparkling or still water?

Wine

el champán ehl chahm•pahn	champagne
el vino... ehl bee•noh...	...wine
– de la casa/de mesa deh lah kah•sah/deh meh•sah	– house/table
– espumoso ehs•poo•moh•soh	– sparkling
– seco/dulce seh•koh/dool•seh	– dry/sweet
– tinto/blanco teen•toh/blahn•koh	– red/white

Mexican wine is produced in the northern part of the country, with the state of Baja California being the best producer.

Wine routes can be followed in northern Mexico—about 50 wineries, from small family-owned to mass producers, can be visited. Tours of the winery and vineyards may be available and some may have on-site restaurants and shops.

Menu Reader

el aceite ehl ah•seyee•teh	oil
el aceite de oliva ehl ah•seyee•teh deh oh•lee•bah	olive oil
la acelga lah ah•sehl•gah	chard

la achicoria lah ah•chee•koh•reeyah chicory

el agua ehl ah•gwah water

el agua quina ehl ah•gwa kee•nah tonic water

el aguacate ehl ah•gwah•kah•teh avocado

el ajo ehl ah•khoh garlic

el ajonjolí ehl ah•khohn•kho•lee sesame

la albahaca lah ahl•bah•kah basil

la alcachofa lah ahl•kah•choh•fah artichoke

la alcaparra lah ahl•kah•pah•rrah caper

la almeja lah ahl•meh•khah clam

la almendra lah ahl•mehn•drah almond

el almíbar ehl ahl•mee•bahr syrup

la alubia lah ah•loo•beeyah bean

las ancas de rana lahs ahn•kahs deh rrah•nah frog's legs

la anchoa lah ahn•choh•ah anchovy

la angula lah ahn•goo•lah baby eel

el anís ehl ah•nees aniseed

el aperitivo ehl ah•peh•ree•tee•boh appetizer [starter]

el apio ehl ah•peeyoh celery

el arándano ehl ah•rahn•dah•noh blueberry

el arándano rojo ehl ah•rahn•dah•noh rroh•khoh cranberry

el arenque ehl ah•rehn•keh herring

el arroz ehl ah•rrohs rice

el arroz integral ehl ah•rrohs een•teh•grahl whole grain rice

el arroz salvaje ehl ah•rrohs sahl•bah•kheh wild rice

el asado ehl ah•sah•doh roast

el atún ehl ah•toon tuna

la avellana lah ah•beh•yah•nah — hazelnut

la avena lah ah•beh•nah — oatmeal

las aves lahs ah•behs — poultry

el azafrán ehl ah•sah•frahn — saffron

el azúcar ehl ah•soo•kahr — sugar

el bagre ehl bah•greh — catfish

la bebida lah beh•bee•dah — drink

el betabel ehl beh•tah•behl — beet

la berenjena lah beh•rehn•kheh•nah — eggplant [aubergine]

la berraza lah beh•rrah•sah — parsnip

el berro ehl beh•rroh — watercress

el bollo ehl boh•yoh — bun

el brandy ehl brahn•dee — brandy

el brócoli ehl broh•koh•lee — broccoli

los brotes de bambú lohs broh•tehs deh bahm•boo — bamboo shoots

el buñuelo ehl boo•nyweh•loh — fritter

la cabra lah kah•brah — goat

el cabrito ehl kah•bree•toh — young goat

el cacahuate ehl kah•kah•wah•teh — peanut

el café ehl kah•feh — coffee

el café capuchino ehl kah•feh kah•poo•chee•noh — cappuccino

el café espresso ehl kah•feh ehs•preh•soh — espresso

la calabacita lah kah•lah•bah•see•tah — zucchini [courgette]

la calabaza lah kah•lah•bah•sah — pumpkin

el calamar ehl kah•lah•mahr — squid

el caldo ehl kahl•doh	broth
caldo tlalpeño kahl•doh tlahl•peh•nyo	soup made with vegetables, chicken and sometimes rice
los callos de hacha lohs kah•yohs deh ah•chah	scallop
el camarón ehl kah•mah•rohn	shrimp
el camote lah kah•moh•teh	yam
la canela lah kah•neh•lah	cinnamon
el cangrejo ehl kahn•greh•khoh	crab
el cangrejo gigante ehl kahn•greh•khoh khee•gahn•teh	spider crab
el caramelo ehl kah•rah•meh•loh	candy [sweet]
la carne lah kahr•neh	meat
la carne de cangrejo lah kahr•neh deh kahn•greh•khoh	crabmeat
la carne de puerco lah kahr•neh deh pwehr•koh	pork
la carne de res lah kahr•neh deh rehs	beef
la carne de venado lah kahr•neh deh beh•nah•doh	venison
la carne molida lah kahr•neh moh•lee•dah	ground beef
las carnes frías lahs kahr•nehs free•ahs	cold cuts [charcuterie]
el carnero ehl kahr•neh•roh	mutton
casero kah•seh•roh	homemade
la castaña lah kahs•tah•nyah	chestnut
el cazón ehl kah•sohn	baby shark
la cebolla lah seh•boh•yah	onion

el cebollín elh seh•boh•yeen	chives
la cebollita de rabo lah seh•boh•yee•tah deh rrah•boh	scallion [spring onion]
la cecina de res lah seh•see•nah deh rrehs	corned beef
el centeno ehl sehn•teh•noh	rye
el cereal ehl seh•reh•ahl	cereal
la cereza lah seh•reh•sah	cherry
la cerveza lah sehr•beh•sah	beer
el chalote ehl chah•loh•teh	shallot
las chalupas lahs chah•loo•pahs	tortillas with potato, chicken, onion and salsa toppings
el champán ehl chahm•pahn	champagne
el champiñón ehl chahm•pee•nyohn	mushroom
el chícharo ehl chee•chah•roh	green pea
el chicharrón ehl chee•chah•rrohn	deep fried pork skin
el chile ehl chee•leh	hot pepper
el chile chipotle ehl chee•leh chee•poh•tleh	chipotle pepper
el chile jalapeño ehl chee•leh khah•lah•peh•nyo	jalapeño pepper
el chile piquín ehl chee•leh pee•keen	powdered red chili pepper
el chile relleno ehl chee•leh reh•yeh•noh	stuffed pepper
el chile verde ehl chee•leh behr•deh	green pepper
la chirivía lah chee•ree•bee•ah	parsnip
el chocolate ehl choh•koh•lah•teh	chocolate
el chocolate caliente ehl choh•koh•lah•teh kah•leeyehn•teh	hot chocolate

la chuleta lah choo•leh•tah	chop
la cigala lah see•gah•lah	crayfish
el cilantro eh see•lahn•troh	coriander
la ciruela lah see•rweh•lah	plum
la ciruela pasa lah see•rweh•lah pah•sah	prune
el clavo de olor ehl klah•boh deh oh•lohr	clove
el coco ehl koh•koh	coconut
la codorniz lah koh•dohr•nees	quail
la col lah kohl	cabbage
la col berza lah kohl behr•sah	kale
la col morada lah kohl moh•rah•dah	red cabbage
la cola de buey lah koh•lah deh booehee	oxtail
las coles de Bruselas lahs koh•lehs deh broo•seh•lahs	Brussels sprouts
la coliflor lah koh•lee•flohr	cauliflower
el comino ehl koh•mee•noh	cumin
la compota lah kohm•poh•tah	stewed fruit
con alcohol kohn ahl•kohl	with alcohol
con crema kohn kreh•mah	with cream
el condimento ehl kohn•dee•mehn•toh	relish
el conejo ehl koh•neh•khoh	rabbit
el congrio ehl kohn•greeyoh	conger eel
los conos lohs koh•nohs	cone
las conservas lahs kohnr•sehr•bahs	pickled
el coñac ehl koh•nyahk	brandy
el corazón ehl koh•rah•sohn	heart
el cordero ehl kohr•deh•roh	lamb

crema creh•mah	soup made with cream and assorted ingredients
la crema agria lah kreh•mah ah•greeyah	sour cream
la crema batida lah kreh•mah bah•tee•dah	whipped cream
crudo kroo•doh	raw
el cuernito ehl kwehr•nee•toh	croissant
los dátiles lohs dah•tee•lehs	dates
descafeinado dehs•kah•feh•ee•nah•doh	decaffeinated
la dona lah doh•nah	doughnut
el durazno ehl doo•rahs•noh	peach
los ejotes lohs eh•khoh•tehs	green beans
la endivia lah ehn•dee•beeyah	endive
el endulzante artificial ehl ehn•dool•sahn•teh ahr•tee•fee•seeyahl	artificial sweetener
el eneldo ehl eh•nehl•doh	dill
la ensalada lah ehn•sah•lah•dah	salad
el espagueti ehl ehs•pah•geh•tee	spaghetti
la espaldilla lah ehs•pahl•dee•yah	shoulder
el espárrago ehl ehs•pah•rrah•goh	asparagus
las especias lahs ehs•peh•seeyahs	spices
la espinaca lah ehs•pee•nah•kah	spinach
el estragón ehl ehs•trah•gohn	tarragon
el faisán ehl fahyee•sahn	pheasant
la falda lah fahl•dah	beef brisket
el fideo ehl fee•deh•oh	noodle

el filete ehl fee•leh•teh	steak
el flan ehl flahn	caramel custard
la fresa lah freh•sah	strawberry
los frijoles refritos lohs free•khoh•lehs rreh•free•tohs	mashed and fried black beans
la fruta lah froo•tah	fruit
los frutos secos lohs froo•tohs seh•kohs	nuts
la galleta lah gah•yeh•tah	cookie [biscuit]
la galleta salada lah gah•yeh•tah sah•lah•dah	cracker
el ganso ehl gahn•soh	wild goose
el garbanzo ehl gahr•bahn•soh	chickpea
el germinado de soya ehl khehr•mee•nah•doh deh soh•yah	bean sprouts
la ginebra lah khee•neh•brah	gin
las gorditas lahs gohr•dee•tahs	little corn cakes baked or fried
la granada roja lah grah•nah•dah roh•khah	pomegranate
la granola lah grah•noh•lah	granola [muesli]
la grosella espinosa lah groh•seh•yah ehs•pee•noh•sah	gooseberry
la grosella negra lah groh•seh•yah neh•grah	black currant
la grosella roja lah groh•seh•yah roh•khah	red currant
el guacamole ehl gwah•kah•moh•leh	mashed avocado, onions, tomatoes and lime juice
la guayaba lah gwah•yah•bah	guava
la guinda lah geen•dah	sour cherry

la hamburguesa lah ahm•boor•geh•sah hamburger

la harina lah ah•ree•nah flour

la harina de maíz lah ah•ree•nah deh mah•ees cornmeal

el helado ehl eh•lah•doh ice cream

el (cubito de) hielo ehl (kooh•bee•toh deh) eeyeh•loh ice (cube)

el hígado ehl ee•gah•doh liver

el higo ehl ee•goh fig

el hinojo ehl ee•noh•khoh fennel

la hoja de laurel lah oh•khah deh lah•oo•rehl bay leaf

el hot dog ehl khot dohg hot dog

el hueso ehl weh•soh bone

el huevo ehl weh•boh egg

el jabalí ehl khah•bah•lee wild boar

la jalea lah khah•leh•ah jelly

el jamón ehl khah•mohn ham

el jengibre ehl khehn•khee•breh ginger

el jerez ehl kheh•rehs sherry

el jitomate ehl khee•toh•mah•teh tomato

el jocoque ehl khoh•koh•keh buttermilk

el jugo ehl khoo•goh juice

el kiwi ehl kee•wee kiwi

la langosta lah lahn•gohs•tah lobster

el langostino ehl lahn•gohs•tee noh prawn

la leche lah leh•cheh milk

la leche de soya lah leh•cheh deh soh•yah soymilk [soya milk]

el lechón ehl leh·chohn — suckling pig

la lechuga lah leh·choo·gah — lettuce

la lengua lah lehn·gwah — tongue

el lenguado ehl lehn·gwah·doh — sole

la lenteja lah lehn·teh·khah — lentil

el licor ehl lee·kohr — liqueur

el licor de naranja ehl lee·kohr deh nah·rahn·khah — orange liqueur

los licores lohs lee·kohr·ehs — spirits

la liebre lah leeyeh·breh — hare

el limón ehl lee·mohn — lime

el limón amarillo ehl lee·mohn ah·mah·ree·yoh — lemon

la limonada lah leeh·moh·nah·dah — lemonade

el lomo ehl loh·moh — loin

la lubina lah loo·bee·nah — sea bass

los macarrones lohs mah·kah·rroh·nehs — macaroni

el maíz ehl mah·ees — sweet corn

la malteada lah mahl·teh·ah·dah — milk shake

la mandarina lah mahn·dah·ree·nah — tangerine

el mango ehl mahn·goh — mango

la mantequilla lah mahn·teh·kee·yah — butter

la manzana lah mahn·sah·nah — apple

la margarina lah mahr·gah·ree·nah — margarine

el marisco ehl mah·rees·koh — shellfish

la mayonesa lah mah·yoh·neh·sah — mayonnaise

el mazapán ehl mah•sah•pahn — marzipan
el mejillón ehl meh•khee•yohn — mussel
la mejorana lah meh•khoh•rah•nah — marjoram
la melaza lah meh•lah•sah — molasses
el melón ehl meh•lohn — melon
la menta lah mehn•tah — mint
las menudencias lahs meh•noo•dehn•seeyahs — giblet
el merengue ehl meh•rehn•geh — meringue
la merluza lah mehr•loo•sah — hake
la mermelada lah mehr•meh•lah•dah — marmalade/jam
el mero ehl meh•roh — grouper
la miel lah meeyehl — honey
la mojarra lah moh•khah•rrah — sea bream
la molleja lah moh•yeh•khah — sweetbread
la morcilla lah mohr•see•yah — black pudding
la mostaza lah mohs•tah•sah — mustard
el nabo ehl nah•boh — turnip
la naranja lah nah•rahn•khah — orange
las natillas lahs nah•tee•yahs — custard
la nieve lah nee•eh•beh — sorbet
la nuez lah nwehs — pecan
la nuez moscada lah nwehs mohs•kah•dah — nutmeg
el omelet ehl oh•meh•leht — omelet
el oporto ehl oh•pohr•toh — port
el orégano ehl oh•reh•gah•noh — oregano
la ostra lah ohs•trah — oyster

la paella lah pah•eh•yah	rice dish
la paletilla lah pah•leh•tee•yah	shank
el palmito ehl pahl•mee•toh	palm heart
el pan ehl pahn	bread
el pan tostado ehl pahn tohs•tah•doh	toast
el panecillo ehl pah•neh•see•yoh	roll
la pancita lah pahn•see•tah	tripe
la papa lah pah•pah	potato
las papas fritas lahs pah•pahs free•tahs	French fries [chips], potato chips [crisps]
la papaya lah pah•pah•yah	papaya
la paprika lah pah•pree•kah	paprika
la pasa lah pah•sah	raisin
la pasta lah pahs•tah	pasta
la pasta de repostería lah pahs•tah deh reh•pohs•teh•ree•ah	pastry
el pastel ehl pahs•tehl	cake
la pata lah pah•tah	leg
las patas de puerco lahs pah•tahs deh pwehr•koh	pig's feet [trotters]
el paté ehl pah•teh	pâté
el pato ehl pah•toh	duck
el pato salvaje ehl pah•toh sahl•bah•kheh	wild duck
el pavo ehl pah•boh	turkey
la pechuga (de pollo) lah peh•choo•gah (deh poh•yoh)	breast (of chicken)
el pejesapo ehl peh•kheh•sah•poh	monkfish

el pepinillo ehl peh•pee•nee•yoh	pickle
el pepino ehl peh•pee•noh	cucumber
la pera lah peh•rah	pear
la perdiz lah pehr•dees	partridge
el perejil ehl peh•reh•kheel	parsley
el pescadito ehl pehs•kah•dee•toh	small fish
el pescado ehl pehs•kah•doh	fish
el pescado frito ehl pehs•kah•doh free•toh	fried fish
pescados y mariscos pehs•kah•dohs ee mah•rees•kohs	seafood
el pez espada ehl pes ehs•pah•dah	swordfish
el pichón ehl pee•chohn	young pigeon
el pie ehl pahee	pie
el pie de queso ehl pahee deh keh•soh	cheesecake
pilsner peelz•nehr	pilsner (beer)
el pimentón dulce ehl pee•mehn•tohn dool•seh	paprika
la pimienta lah pee•meeyehn•tah	pepper (seasoning)
la pimienta negra lah pee•meeyehn•tah neh•grah	black pepper
el pimiento ehl pee•meeyehn•toh	pepper (vegetable)
la piña lah pee•nyah	pineapple
los piñones lohs pee•nyohn•ehs	pine nuts
la pizza lah peet•sah	pizza
el plátano ehl plah•tah•noh	banana
el pollo ehl poh•yoh	chicken
el pollo frito ehl poh•yoh free•toh	fried chicken

el poro ehl poh·roh	leek
el pozole poh·soh·leh	soup of stewed pork and corn kernels, garnished with lettuce, horseradish and oregano
el pulpo ehl pool·poh	octopus
las quesadillas lahs keh·sah·dee·yahs	corn tortillas stuffed with cheese, beef, chicken, etc.
el queso ehl keh·soh	cheese
el queso fundido ehl keh·soh foon·dee·doh	Mexican fondue
el rábano ehl rrah·bah·noh	radish
el raspado ehl rrahs·pah·doh	fruit flavored iced drink
los ravioles lohs rrah·beeyoh·lehs	ravioli
la raya lah rrah·yah	skate
el refresco ehl rreh·frehs·koh	soda
relleno rreh·yehn·noh	stuffed/stuffing
el requesón ehl rreh·keh·sohn	similar to ricotta cheese
la res lah rrehs	beef
el riñón ehl rree·nyohn	kidney
el romero ehl rroh·meh·roh	rosemary
el ron ehl rrohn	rum
rubia rroo·beeyah	lager (beer)
el ruibarbo ehl rrooee·bahr·boh	rhubarb
la sal lah sahl	salt

el salami ehl sah•lah•mee	salami
la salchicha lah sahl•chee•chah	sausage
el salmón ehl sahl•mohn	salmon
el salmonete ehl sahl•moh•neh•teh	red mullet
la salsa lah sahl•sah	chopped or pureed tomatoes, chiles, raw onions and cilantro
la salsa agridulce lah sahl•sah ah•gree•dool•seh	sweet and sour sauce
la salsa al mojo de ajo lah sahl•sah ahl moh•khoh deh ah•kho	garlic sauce
la salsa catsup lah sahl•sah kaht•soop	ketchup
la salsa de soya lah sahl•sah deh soh•yah	soy sauce
la salsa picante lah sahl•sah pee•kahn•teh	hot pepper sauce
la salvia lah sahl•beeyah	sage
la sandía lah sahn•dee•ah	watermelon
el sándwich ehl sahnd•weech	sandwich
la sangría lah sahn•gree•ah	wine punch
la sardina lah sahr•dee•nah	sardine
el sazonador ehl sah•soh•nah•dohr	allspice
la semilla lah seh•mee•yah	seed
la semilla de soya lah seh•mee•yah deh soh•yah	soybean [soya bean]
los sesos lohs seh•sohs	brains
la sidra lah see•drah	cider
el sirloin ehl seer•loh•een	sirloin

la sopa lah soh•pah | soup

sopa de lima soh•pah deh lee•mah | lima (citrus fruit) soup with seasoned chicken broth

sopa de tortilla soh•pah deh tohr•tee•yah | tomato broth garnished with fried tortilla strips, cream, avocado, cheese, chile and pork skin

la soya lah soh•yah | soy [soya]

el T-bone ehl tee•bohn | T-bone

los tacos lohs tah•kohs | soft tortillas filled with a variety of meat and vegetables

el té ehl teh | tea

la ternera lah tehr•neh•rah | veal

el tequila ehl teh•kee•lah | tequila

el tiburón ehl tee•boo•rohn | shark

tinto teen•toh | red (wine)

el tocino ehl toh•see•noh | bacon

el tomillo ehl toh•mee•yoh | thyme

la toronja lah toh•rohn•khah | grapefruit

la tortilla lah tohr•tee•yah | thin, flat bread made of corn

el trigo ehl tree•goh | wheat

las tripas lahs tree•pahs | organ meat [offal]

la trucha lah troo•chah | trout

las trufas lahs troo•fahs | truffles

Talking

Essential

Hello!	**¡Hola!** oh·lah
How are you?	**¿Cómo estás?** koh·moh ehs·tahs
Fine, thanks.	**Bien, gracias.** beeyehn grah·seeyahs
Excuse me!	**¡Disculpe!** dihs·koohl·peh
Do you speak English?	**¿Habla inglés?** ah·blah een·glehs
What's your name?	**¿Cómo se llama?** koh·moh seh yah·mah
My name is…	**Me llamo…** meh yah·moh…
Nice to meet you.	**Encantado♂/Encantada♀.** ehn·kahn·tah·doh♂/ehn·kahn·tah·dah♀
Where are you from?	**¿De dónde es usted?** deh dohn·deh es oos·tehd
I'm from the *U.S./U.K.*	**Soy *de Estados Unidos/del Reino Unido.*** soy *deh ehs·tah·dohs oo·nee·dohs/dehl rreyee·noh oo·nee·doh*
What do you do?	**¿A qué se dedica?** ah keh seh deh·dee·kah
I work for…	**Trabajo para…** trah·bah·khoh pah·rah…
I'm a student.	**Soy estudiante.** soy ehs·too·deeyahn·teh
I'm retired.	**Estoy jubilado♂/jubilada♀.** ehs·toy khoo·bee·lah·doh♂/khoo·bee·lah·dah♀
Do you like…?	**¿Le gusta…?** leh goos·tah…
Goodbye.	**Adiós.** ah·deeyohs
See you later.	**Hasta luego.** ah·stah lweh·goh

In Spanish, there are a number of forms for "you", taking different verb forms: **tú** (singular, informal), **usted** (singular, formal) and **ustedes** (plural). When addressing strangers, always use the more formal **usted** (singular) as opposed to the more familiar **tú** (singular), until told otherwise.

If you know someone's professional title, it's polite to use it, e.g., **doctor** (male doctor), **doctora** (female doctor). You can also simply say **Señor** (Mr.), **Señora** (Mrs.) or **Señorita** (Miss).

Communication Difficulties

Do you speak English?	**¿Habla inglés?** ah•blah een•glehs
Does anyone here speak English?	**¿Hay alguien que hable inglés?** aye ahl•geeyen keh ah•bleh een•glehs
I don't speak (much) Spanish.	**No hablo (mucho) español.** noh ah•bloh (moo•choh) ehs•pah•nyol
Can you speak more slowly?	**¿Puede hablar más despacio?** pweh•deh ah•blahr mahs dehs•pah•seeyoh
Can you repeat that?	**¿Podría repetir eso?** poh•dree•ah rreh•peh•teer eh•soh
Excuse me?	**¿Cómo?** koh•moh

What was that?	**¿Qué dijo?** keh dee•khoh
Can you spell it?	**¿Cómo se escribe?** koh•moh seh ehs•kree•beh
Please write it down.	**Escríbamelo, por favor.** ehs•kree•bah•meh•loh pohr fah•bohr
Can you translate this into English for me?	**¿Podría traducirme esto al inglés?** poh•dree•ah trah•doo•seer•meh ehs•toh ahl een•glehs
What does *this/that* mean?	**¿Qué significa *esto/eso*?** keh seeg•nee•fee•kah *ehs•toh/eh•soh*
I understand.	**Entiendo.** ehn•teeyehn•doh
I don't understand.	**No entiendo.** noh ehn•teeyehn•doh
Do you understand?	**¿Entiende?** ehn•teeyehn•deh

You May Hear…

Hablo muy poco inglés. ah•bloh mooy poh•koh een•glehs	I only speak a little English.
No hablo inglés. noh ah•bloh een•glehs	I don't speak English.

Making Friends

Hello!	**¡Hola!** oh•lah
Good morning.	**Buenos días.** bweh•nohs dee•ahs
Good afternoon.	**Buenas tardes.** bweh•nahs tahr•dehs
Good evening.	**Buenas noches.** bweh•nahs noh•chehs
My name is…	**Me llamo…** meh yah•moh…
What's your name?	**¿Cómo te llamas?** koh•moh teh yah•mahs
I'd like to introduce you to…	**Quiero presentarle a…** keeyeh•roh preh•sehn•tahr•leh ah…

Nice to meet you.	**Encantado♂/Encantada♀.** ehn•kahn•tah•doh♂/ehn•kahn•tah•dah♀
How are you?	**¿Cómo estás?** koh•moh ehs•tahs
Fine, thanks. And you?	**Bien gracias. ¿Y usted?** beeyehn grah•seeyahs ee oos•tehd

When meeting someone for the first time in Mexico greet him or her with **hola** (hello), **buenos días** (good morning), **buenas tardes** (good afternoon) or **buenas noches** (good evening). Mexicans even extend this general greeting to strangers when in elevators, waiting rooms and other small public spaces. A general acknowledgment or reply is expected from all. When leaving, say **adiós** (goodbye).

Travel Talk

I'm here...	**Estoy aquí...** ehs•toy ah•kee...
– on business	**– en viaje de negocios** ehn beeyah•kheh deh neh•goh•seeyohs
– on vacation	**– de vacaciones** deh bah•kah•seeyoh•nehs [holiday]
– studying	**– estudiando** ehs•too•deeyahn•doh
I'm staying for...	**Voy a quedarme...** boy ah keh•dahr•meh...
I've been here...	**Llevo aquí...** yeh•boh ah•kee...
– a day	**– un día** oon dee•ah
– a week	**– una semana** oo•nah seh•mah•nah
– a month	**– un mes** oon mehs

▶For numbers, see page 178.

Where are you from?	**¿De dónde es?** deh dohn•deh ehs
I'm from...	**Soy de...** soy deh...

Relationships

Who are you with? **¿Con quién vino?** kohn keeyehn beeh·noh

I'm here alone. **Vine solo♂/sola♀.** beeh·neh soh·loh♂/soh·lah♀

I'm with my... **Vine con mi...** beeh·neh kohn mee...

– husband/wife **– esposo♂/esposa♀** ehs·poh·soh♂/ehs·poh·sah♀

– boyfriend/girlfriend **– novio♂/novia♀** noh·beeyoh♂/noh·beeyah♀

– friend(s)/colleague(s) **– amigo(s)/colega(s)** ah·mee·goh(s)/koh·leh·gah(s)

When's your birthday? **¿Cuándo es su cumpleaños?** kwahn·doh ehs soo koom·pleh·ah·nyohs

How old are you? **¿Cuántos años tiene?** kwahntohs ahn·yos teeyeh·neh

I'm... **Tengo...años.** tehn·goh...ah·nyohs

►For numbers, see page 178.

Are you married? **¿Está casado♂/casada♀?** ehs·tah kah·sah·doh♂/kah·sah·dah♀

I'm... **Estoy...** ehs·toy...

– single **– soltero♂/soltera♀** sohl·teh·roh♂/sohl·teh·rah♀

– in a relationship **– en una relación** ehn oo·nah rreh·lah·seeyohn

– married **– casado♂/casada♀** kah·sah·doh♂/kah·sah·dah♀

– divorced **– divorciado♂/divorciada♀** dee·bohr·seeyah·doh♂/dee·bohr·seeyah·dah♀

– separated **– separado♂/separada♀** seh·pah·rah·doh♂/seh·pah·rah·dah♀

I'm widowed. **Soy viudo♂/viuda♀.** soy beeyoo·doh♂/beeyoo·dah♀

Do you have *children/ grandchildren*?	**¿Tiene *hijos/nietos*?** teeyeh•neh *ee•khohs/neeyeh•tohs*

Work and School

What do you do?	**¿A qué se dedica?** ah keh seh deh•dee•kah
What are you studying?	**¿Qué estudia?** keh ehs•too•deeyah
I'm studying Spanish.	**Estudio español.** ehs•too•deeyoh ehs•pah•nyohl
I...	**Yo...** yoh...
– work *full-time/ part-time*	**– trabajo *a tiempo completo/medio tiempo*** trah•bah•khoh *ah teeyehm•poh kohm•pleh•toh/meh•deeoh teeyehm•poh*
– am unemployed	**– estoy desempleado** ehs•toy dehs•ehm•pleh•ah•doh
– work at home	**– trabajo desde casa** trah•bah•khoh dehz•deh kah•sah
Who do you work for?	**¿Para quién trabaja?** pah•rah keeyehn trah•bah•khah
I work for...	**Trabajo para...** trah•bah•khoh pah•rah...
Here's my business card.	**Aquí tiene mi tarjeta.** ah•kee teeyeh•neh mee tahr•kheh•tah

▶For business travel, see page 152.

Weather

What's the forecast?	**¿Cuál es el pronóstico del tiempo?** kwahl ehs ehl proh•nohs•tee•koh dehl teeyehm•poh
What *beautiful/ terrible* weather!	**¡Qué clima más *bonito/feo* hace!** keh clee•mah mahs *boh•nee•toh/feh•oh* ah•seh

It's *cool/warm.*	**Hace *frío/calor*.** ah·seh *free·oh/kah·lohr*
It's *rainy/sunny.*	**Está *lluvioso/soleado*.** ehs·tah *yoo·beeyoh·soh/soh·leh·ah·doh*
It's *snowy/icy.*	**Hay *nieve/hielo*.** aye *neeyeh·beh/eeyeh·loh*
Do I need *a jacket/ an umbrella*?	**¿Necesito *una chamarra/un paraguas*?** neh·seh·see·toh *oo·nah chah·mah·rrah/ oon pah·rah·gwahs*

▶For temperature, see page 184.

Romance

Essential

Would you like to go out for *a drink/dinner*?	**¿Le gustaría salir a *tomar una copa/cenar*?** leh goos·tah·ree·ah sah·leer ah *toh·mahr oo·nah koh·pah/seh·nahr*
What are your plans for *tonight/ tomorrow*?	**¿Qué planes tiene para *esta noche/ mañana*?** keh plah·nehs teeyeh·neh pah·rah *ehs·tah noh·cheh/mah·nyah·nah*
Can I have your number?	**¿Puede darme su número?** pweh·deh dahr·meh soo noo·meh·roh
Can I join you?	**¿Puedo acompañarlo♂/acompañarla♀?** pweh·doh ah·kohm·pah·nyahr·loh♂/ ah·kohm·pah·nyahr·lah♀
Can I buy you a drink?	**¿Puedo invitarle una copa?** pweh·doh een·bee·tahr·leh oo·nah koh·pah
I like you.	**Me gustas.** meh goos·tahs
I love you.	**Te amo.** teh ah·moh

Making Plans

Would you like to go out for…?	**¿Le gustaría salir a…?** leh goos•tah•ree•ah sah•leer ah…
– coffee	**– tomar un café** toh•mahr oon kah•feh
– dinner	**– cenar** seh•nahr
– a drink	**– tomar una copa** toh•mahr oo•nah koh•pah
What are your plans for…?	**¿Qué va a hacer…?** keh bah ah ah•sehr…
– tonight	**– esta noche** ehs•tah noh•cheh
– tomorrow	**– mañana** mah•nyah•nah
– this weekend	**– este fin de semana** ehs•teh feen deh seh•mah•nah
Where would you like to go?	**¿Adónde le gustaría ir?** ah•dohn•deh leh goos•tah•ree•ah eer
I'd like to go to…	**Me gustaría ir a…** meh goos•tah•ree•ah eer ah…
Do you like…?	**¿Le gusta…?** leh goos•tah…

Can I have your *number/e-mail*?	**¿Puede darme su *número/dirección de correo electrónico*?** pweh•deh dahr•meh soo *noo•meh•roh/dee•rehk•seeyohn deh koh•rreh•oh eh•lehk•troh•nee•koh*

▶For e-mail and phone, see page 50.

Pick-up [Chat-up] Lines

Can I join you?	**¿Puedo acompañarlo♂/acompañarla♀?** pweh•doh ah•kohm•pah•nyahr•loh♂/ ah•kohm•pah•nyahr•lah♀
You're very attractive.	**Es muy guapo♂/guapa♀.** ehs mooy gwah•poh♂/gwah•pah♀
Let's go somewhere quieter.	**Vayamos a un sitio más tranquilo.** bah•yah•mohs ah oon see•teeyoh mahs trahn•kee•loh

Accepting and Rejecting

I'd love to.	**Me encantaría.** meh ehn•kahn•tah•ree•yah
Where should we meet?	**¿Dónde nos vemos?** dohn•deh nohs beh•mohs
I'll meet you at *the bar/your hotel*.	**Nos vemos en *el bar/su hotel*.** nohs beh•mohs ehn *ehl bahr/soo oh•tehl*
I'll come by at...	**Pasaré a...** pah•sah•reh ah...

▶For time, see page 180.

What is your address?	**¿Dónde vive?** dohn•deh bee•beh
I'm busy.	**Estoy ocupado♂/ocupada♀.** ehs•toy oh•koo•pah•doh♂/oh•koo•pah•dah♀
I'm not interested.	**No me interesa.** noh meh een•teh•reh•sah

Leave me alone.	**Déjeme en paz.** deh•kheh•meh ehn pahs
Stop bothering me!	**¡Deje de molestarme!** deh•kheh deh moh•lehs•tahr•meh

Getting Physical

Can I *hug/kiss* you?	**¿Puedo *abrazarte/besarte*?** pweh•doh *ah•brah•sahr•teh/beh•sahr•teh*
Yes.	**Sí.** see
No.	**No.** noh
Stop!	**¡Basta!** bahs•tah

Sexual Preferences

Are you gay?	**¿Es gay?** ehs gay
I'm…	**Soy…** soy…
– heterosexual	**– heterosexual** eh•teh•roh•sex•wahl
– homosexual	**– homosexual** oh•moh•sex•wahl
– bisexual	**– bisexual** bee•sex•wahl
Do you like *men/women*?	**¿Le gustan *los hombres/las mujeres*?** leh goos•tahn *lohs ohm•brehs/lahs moo•kheh•rehs*

▶For informal and formal "you," see page 172.

▼ Fun

Sightseeing

Essential

Where's the tourist information office? **¿Dónde está la oficina de turismo?** dohn•deh ehs•tah lah oh•fee•see•nah deh too•reez•moh

What are the main attractions? **¿Dónde están los principales sitios de interés?** dohn•deh ehs•tahn lohs preen•see•pah•lehs see•teeyohs deh een•teh•rehs

Do you have tours in English? **¿Hay recorridos en inglés?** aye rreh•koh•rree•dohs ehn een•glehs

Can I have a *map/guide*? **¿Puede darme *un mapa/una guía*?** pweh•deh dahr•meh *oon mah•pah/oo•nah gee•ah*

Tourist Information Office

Do you have information on...? **¿Tiene información sobre...?** teeyeh•neh een•fohr•mah•seeyohn soh•breh...

Can you recommend...? **¿Puede recomendarme...?** pweh•deh rreh•koh•mehn•dahr•meh...

– a bus tour **– un recorrido en camión** oon rreh•koh•rree•doh ehn kah•meeyohn

– an excursion to... **– una excursión a...** oo•nah ehx•koor•seeyohn ah...

– a sightseeing tour **– un recorrido turístico** oon rreh•koh•rree•doh too•rees•tee•koh

i Tourist offices are located in major Mexican cities and in many of the smaller towns that are popular tourist attractions. They work regular business hours Monday–Friday; on Saturday and Sunday, they typically open with a more restricted schedule. Information can also be found via the Mexican Tourism Board's official website.

▶For useful websites, see page 185.

Tours

I'd like to go on the tour to...	**Quiero ir al recorrido de...** keeyeh•roh eer ahl rreh•koh•rree•doh deh...
When's the next tour?	**¿Cuándo es el próximo recorrido?** kwahn•doh ehs ehl proh•xee•moh rreh•koh•rree•doh
Are there tours in English?	**¿Hay recorridos en inglés?** aye rreh•koh•rree•dohs ehn een•glehs
Is there an English *guide book/audio guide*?	**¿Hay una *guía/audioguía* en inglés?** aye oo•nah *gee•ah/awoo•deeyoh•gee•ah* ehn een•glehs
What time do we *leave/return*?	**¿A qué hora *salimos/regresamos*?** ah keh oh•rah *sah•lee•mohs/rreh•greh•sahm•mohs*
We'd like to see...	**Queremos ver...** keh•reh•mohs behr...
Can we stop here...?	**¿Podemos parar aquí...?** poh•deh•mohs pah•rahr ah•kee...
– to take photos	**– para tomar fotos** pah•rah toh•mahr foh•tohs
– for souvenirs	**– para comprar recuerdos** pah•rah kohm•prahr rreh•kwehr•dohs
– for the restroom [toilet]	**– para ir al baño** pah•rah eer ahl bah•nyo
Is it handicapped [disabled]-accessible?	**¿Tiene acceso para discapacitados?** teeyeh•neh ahk•seh•soh pah•rah dees•kah•pah•see•tah•dohs

▶For ticketing, see page 20.

Sights

Where *is/are*...?	**¿Dónde *está/están*...?** dohn•deh *ehs•tah/ehs•tahn*...
– the battleground	**– el campo de batalla** ehl kahm•poh deh bah•tah•yah
– the beach	**– la playa** lah plah•yah

– the botanical garden	**– el jardín botánico** ehl khahr·deen boh·tah·nee·koh
– the castle	**– el castillo** ehl kahs·tee·yoh
– the cave	**– la cueva** lah kwe·bah
– the downtown area	**– el centro** ehl sehn·troh
– the fountain	**– la fuente** lah fwehn·teh
– the grotto	**– la gruta** lah groo·tah
– the library	**– la biblioteca** lah bee·bleeyoh·teh·kah
– the market	**– el mercado** ehl mehr·kah·doh
– the museum	**– el museo** ehl moo·seh·oh
– the old town	**– el barrio viejo** ehl bah·rryo beeyeh·khoh
– the palace	**– el palacio** ehl pah·lah·seeyoh
– the park	**– el parque** ehl pahr·keh
– the ruins	**– las ruinas** lahs rrwee·nahs
– the shopping area	**– la zona comercial** lahs soh·nah koh·mehr·seeyahl
– the town square	**– la plaza** lah plah·sah
Can you show me on the map?	**¿Puede enseñármelo en el mapa?** pweh·deh ehn·seh·nyahr·meh·loh ehn ehl mah·pah

▶For directions, see page 34.

Impressions

It's...	**Es...** ehs...
– amazing	**– increíble** een·kreh·ee·bleh
– beautiful	**– precioso** preh·seeyoh·soh
– boring	**– aburrido** ah·boo·rree·doh
– interesting	**– interesante** een·teh·reh·sahn·teh
– magnificent	**– magnífico** mahg·nee·fee·koh
– romantic	**– romántico** rroh·mahn·tee·koh
– strange	**– raro** rrah·roh
– stunning	**– impresionante** eem·preh·seeyoh·nahn·teh
– terrible	**– horrible** oh·rree·bleh
– ugly	**– feo** feh·oh
I (don't) like it.	**(No) Me gusta.** (noh) meh goo·stah

Religion

Where is...?	**¿Dónde está...?** dohn·deh ehs·tah...
– the cathedral	**– la catedral** lah kah·teh·drahl
– the *Catholic/Protestant* church	**– la iglesia *católica/protestante*** lah ee·gleh·seeyah *kah·toh·lee·kah/ proh·tehs·tahn·teh*
– the mosque	**– la mezquita** lah mehs·kee·tah
– the shrine	**– el santuario** ehl sahn·twah·reeyoh
– the synagogue	**– la sinagoga** lah see·nah·goh·gah
– the temple	**– el templo** ehl tehm·ploh
What time is *mass/the service*?	**¿A qué hora es *la misa/el servicio*?** ah keh oh·rah ehs *lah mee·sah/ehl sehr·bee·seeyoh*

Shopping

Essential

Where's the *market/ mall [shopping centre]*?	**¿Dónde está el *mercado/centro comercial*?** dohn•deh ehs•tah ehl *mehr•kah•doh/sehn•troh koh•mehr•seeyahl*
I'm just looking.	**Sólo estoy mirando.** soh•loh ehs•toy mee•rahn•doh
Can you help me?	**¿Puede ayudarme?** pweh•deh ah•yoo•dahr•meh
I'm being helped.	**Ya me atienden.** yah meh ah•teeyehn•dehn
How much?	**¿Cuánto es?** kwahn•toh ehs
That one, please.	**Ése ♂/Ésa ♀, por favor.** eh•seh ♂/eh•sah ♀ pohr fah•bohr
That's all.	**Eso es todo.** eh•soh ehs toh•doh
Where can I pay?	**¿Dónde se paga?** dohn•deh seh pah•gah
I'll pay *in cash/by credit card.*	**Voy a pagar *en efectivo/con tarjeta de crédito.*** boy ah pah•gahr *ehn eh•fehk•tee•boh/ kohn tahr•kheh•tah deh kreh•dee•toh*
A receipt, please.	**Un comprobante, por favor.** oon kohm•proh•bahn•teh pohr fah•bohr

Mercados (markets) and **mercados sobre ruedas** (traveling markets) are popular in the cities and towns of Mexico. A wide variety of goods is available at these markets, including fruit and vegetables, antiques, souvenirs, regional items and so on. Your hotel or local tourist office will have information on the markets in your area. Most **mercados** are open daily from early morning until late afternoon; the **mercados sobre ruedas** times vary by location.

Stores

Where *is/are*...?	**¿Dónde *está/están*...?** dohn·deh *ehs·tah/ehs·tahn*...
– the antiques store	**– la tienda de antigüedades** lah teeyehn·dah deh ahn·tee·gweh·dah·dehs
– the bakery	**– la panadería** lah pah·nah·deh·ree·ah
– the bank	**– el banco** ehl bahn·koh
– the bookstore	**– la librería** lah lee·breh·ree·ah
– the clothing store	**– la tienda de ropa** lah teeyehn·dah deh rroh·pah
– the delicatessen	**– la salchichonería** lah sahl·chee·choh·neh·ree·ah
– the department stores	**– las tiendas departamentales** lahs teeyenh·dahs deh·pahr·tah·mehn·tah·lehs
– the gift shop	**– la tienda de regalos** lah teeyehn·dah deh rreh·gah·lohs
– the health food store	**– la tienda de alimentos naturales** lah teeyehn·dah deh ah·lee·mehn·tohs nah·too·rahl·ehs
– the jeweler's	**– la joyería** lah khoh·yeh·ree·ah

– the liquor store [off-licence]	– **la licorería** lah lee•coh•reh•ree•ah
– the market	– **el mercado** ehl mehr•kah•doh
– the pastry shop	– **la pastelería** lah pahs•teh•leh•ree•ah
– the pharmacy [chemist]	– **la farmacia** lah fahr•mah•seeyah
– the produce [grocery] store	– **la tienda de frutas y verduras** lah teeyehn•dah deh froo•tahs ee behr•doo•rahs
– the shoe store	– **la zapatería** lah sah•pah•teh•ree•ah
– the shopping mall [shopping centre]	– **el centro comercial** ehl sehn•troh koh•mehr•seeyahl
– the souvenir store	– **la tienda de recuerdos** lah teeyehn•dah deh rreh•kwehr•dohs
– the supermarket	– **el supermercado** ehl soo•pehr•mehr•kah•doh
– the tobacconist	– **la tabaquería** lah tah•bah•keh•ree•ah
– the toy store	– **la juguetería** lah khoo•geh•teh•ree•ah

Services

Can you recommend...?	**¿Puede recomendarme...?** pweh•deh rreh•koh•mehn•dahr•meh...
– a barber	– **una peluquería** oo•nah peh•loo•keh•ree•ah
– a dry cleaner	– **una tintorería** oo•nah teen•toh•reh•ree•ah
– a hairstylist	– **un salón de belleza** oon sah•lohn deh beh•yeh•sah
– a laundromat [launderette]	– **una lavandería** oo•nah lah•bahn•deh•ree•ah
– a nail salon	– **el manicurista** ehl mah•nee•koo•rees•tah
– a spa	– **spa** ehs•pah

Can you…this?	**¿Puede…esto?** pweh·deh…ehs·toh
– alter	**– hacerle un arreglo a** ah·sehr·leh oon ah·rreh·gloh ah
– clean	**– limpiar** leem·peeyahr
– fix [mend]	**– zurcir** soor·seer
– press	**– planchar** plahn·chahr
When will it be ready?	**¿Cuándo estará listo?** kwahn·doh ehs·tah·rah lees·toh

Spa

I'd like…	**Quiero…** keeyeh·roh…
– an *eyebrow/ a bikini* wax	**– depilarme las *cejas/ingles*** deh·pee·lahr·meh lahs *seh·khahs/een·glehs*
– a facial	**– hacerme un facial** ah·sehr·meh oon fah·seeyahl
– a *manicure/ pedicure*	**– hacerme el *manicure/pedicure*** ah·sehr·meh ehl *mah·nee·koo·reh/ peh·dee·koo·reh*
– a (sports) massage	**– un masaje (deportivo)** oon mah·sah·kheh (deh·pohr·tee·boh)
Do you do…?	**¿Hacen…?** ah·sehn…
– acupuncture	**– acupuntura** ah·koo·poon·too·rah
– aromatherapy	**– aromaterapia** ah·roh·mah·teh·rah·peeyah
– oxygen treatment	**– oxígenoterapia** oh·xee·kheh·noh·teh·rah·peeyah
Do you have a sauna?	**¿Tienen un sauna?** teeyeh·nehn oon sawoo·nah

Mexico has many spas, wellness centers and health-based resorts. These facilities offer a wide selection of treatments, including relaxation therapies and herbal remedies. Resort and overnight spas often offer individual services to those not staying there. Many of these also offer other leisure activities such as horseback riding, guided tours, golf and swimming. Some spas and resorts do not allow children, so check before booking if you are traveling with kids.

▶For useful websites, see page 185.

Hair Salon

I'd like...	**Quiero...** keeyeh•roh...
– an appointment for *today/tomorrow*	**– hacer cita para *hoy/mañana*** ah•sehr see•tah pah•rah *oy/mah•nyah•nah*
– some color	**– pintarme el pelo** peen•tahr•meh ehl peh•loh
– some highlights	**– hacerme luces** ah•sehr•meh loo•sehs
– my hair styled	**– hacerme un peinado** ah•sehr•meh oon peyee•nah•doh
– a haircut	**– cortarme el pelo** kohr•tahr•meh ehl peh•loh
– a trim	**– cortarme las puntas** kohr•tahr•meh lahs poon•tahs
Not too short.	**No me lo corte demasiado.** noh meh loh kohr•teh deh•mah•seeyah•doh
Shorter here.	**Quíteme más de aquí.** kee•teh•meh mahs deh ah•kee

Sales Help

When do you *open/close*?	**¿A qué hora *abren/cierran*?** ah keh oh•rah *ah•brehn/seeyeh•rrahn*
Where *is/are*...?	**¿Dónde *está/están*...?** dohn•deh *ehs•tah/ehs•tahn*...
– the cashier	**– la caja** lah kah•khah
– the escalators	**– las escaleras eléctricas** lahs ehs•kah•leh•rahs eh•lehk•tree•kahs
– the elevator [lift]	**– el elevador** ehl eh•leh•bah•dohr
– the fitting room	**– el probador** ehl proh•bah•dohr
– the store directory	**– la guía de tiendas** lah gee•ah deh teeyehn•dahs
Can you help me?	**¿Puede ayudarme?** pweh•deh ah•yoo•dahr•meh
I'm just looking.	**Sólo estoy mirando.** soh•loh ehs•toy mee•rahn•doh
I'm being helped.	**Ya me atienden.** yah meh ah•teeyehn•dehn
Do you have...?	**¿Tienen...?** teeyeh•nehn...
Can you show me...?	**¿Podría enseñarme...?** poh•dree•ah ehn•seh•nyahr•meh...
Can you *ship/wrap* it?	**¿Pueden *hacer un envío/envolverlo*?** pweh•dehn *ah•sehr oon ehn•bee•oh/ehn•bohl•behr•loh*
How much?	**¿Cuánto es?** kwahn•toh ehs
That's all.	**Eso es todo.** eh•soh ehs toh•doh

▶For clothing items, see page 136.

▶For food items, see page 90.

▶For souvenirs, see page 132.

You May Hear...

¿Necesita ayuda? neh•seh•see•tah ah•yoo•dah	Can I help you?
Un momento. oon moh•mehn•toh	One moment.
¿Qué desea? keh deh•seh•ah	What would you like?
¿Algo más? ahl•goh mahs	Anything else?

Preferences

I'd like something...	**Quiero algo...** keeyeh•roh ahl•goh...
– cheap/expensive	**– barato/caro** bah•rah•toh/kah•roh
– from this region	**– de esta región** deh ehs•tah rreh•kheeyohn
– larger/smaller	**– más grande/más pequeño** mahs grahn•deh/mahs peh•keh•nyoh
Around...pesos.	**De unos...pesos.** deh oo•nohs...peh•sohs
Is it real?	**¿Es auténtico♂/auténtica♀?** ehs awoo•tehn•tee•koh♂/awoo•tehn•tee•kah♀
Can you show me *this/that*?	**¿Puede mostrarme *esto/eso*?** pweh•deh mohs•trahr•meh *ehs•toh/eh•soh*

▶For currency, see page 18.

▶For numbers, see page 178.

Decisions

That's not quite what I want.	**Eso no es realmente lo que busco.** eh•soh noh ehs rreh•ahl•mehn•teh loh keh boos•koh
No, I don't like it.	**No, no me gusta.** noh noh meh goos•tah
It's too expensive.	**Es demasiado caro.** ehs deh•mah•seeyah•doh kah•roh
I have to think about it.	**Voy a pensarlo.** boy ah pehn•sahr•loh
I'll take it.	**Me lo llevo.** meh loh yeh•boh

Bargaining

That's too much. **Eso es mucho.** eh•soh ehs moo•choh

I'll give you… **Le doy…** leh doy…

I have only… pesos. **Sólo tengo…pesos.** soh•loh tehn•goh…peh•sohs

Is that your best price? **¿Es el mejor precio que me puede hacer?** ehs ehl meh•khohr preh•seeyoh keh meh pweh•deh ah•sehr

Can you give me a discount? **¿En cuánto me lo deja?** ehn kwahn•toh meh loh deh•khah

▶For numbers, see page 178.

▶For currency, see page 18.

You May Hear…

¿Cómo va a pagar? koh•moh bah ah pah•gahr — How are you paying?

Rechazaron su tarjeta. rreh•chah•sah•rohn soo tahr•kheh•tah — Your credit card has been declined.

Su identificación, por favor. soo ee•dehn•tee•fee•kah•seeyohn pohr fah•bohr — ID, please.

No aceptamos tarjetas de crédito. noh ah•sehp•tah•mohs tahr•kheh•tahs deh kreh•dee•toh — We don't accept credit cards.

Sólo en efectivo, por favor. soh•loh ehn eh•fehk•tee•boh pohr fah•bohr — Cash only, please.

¿Tiene *cambio/billetes más chicos*? teeyeh•neh *kahm•beeyoh/bee•yeh•tehs mahs chee•kohs* — Do you have *change/small bills [notes]*?

Paying

How much?	**¿Cuánto es?** kwahn•toh ehs
I'll pay…	**Voy a pagar…** boy ah pah•gahr…
– in cash	**– en efectivo** ehn eh•fehk•tee•boh
– by credit card	**– con tarjeta de crédito** kohn tahr•kheh•tah deh kreh•dee•toh
– by traveler's check [cheque]	**– con cheque de viajero** kohn cheh•keh deh beeyah•kheh•roh
A receipt, please.	**Un comprobante, por favor.** oon kohm•proh•bahn•teh pohr fah•bohr

Tarjetas de crédito (credit cards) are widely accepted throughout Mexico; you may need to show ID when using a credit card. Mastercard™ and Visa™ are the most commonly used; American Express® is accepted in most places. **Tarjetas de débito** (debit cards) are also common; these are usually accepted if backed by Visa™ or Mastercard™. Traveler's checks are not accepted everywhere; have an alternative form of payment available. Cash is the preferred method of payment—some places, such as chain convenience stores, newsstands, tobacconists, flower shops and market or street vendors take cash only.

Complaints

I'd like…	**Quiero…** keeyeh•roh…
– a refund	**– que me devuelvan el dinero** keh meh deh•bwehl•bahn ehl dee•neh•roh
– to exchange this	**– cambiar esto por otro** kahm•beeyahr ehs•toh pohr oh•troh
– to return this	**– devolver esto** deh•bohl•behr ehs•toh
– to speak to the manager	**– hablar con el encargado** ah•blahr kohn ehl ehn•kahr•gah•doh

Souvenirs

ashtrays	**los ceniceros** lohs seh•nee•seh•rohs
bottle of wine	**la botella de vino** lah boh•teh•yah deh bee•noh
box of chocolates	**la caja de chocolates** lah kah•khah deh choh•koh•lah•tehs
Charro hat	**el sombrero de charro** ehl sohm•breh•roh deh chah•rroh
fan (wooden)	**el abanico de madera** ehl ah•bah•nee•koh deh mah•deh•rah
key ring	**el llavero** ehl yah•beh•roh
Mexican doll	**la muñeca mexicana** lah moo•nyeh•kah meh•khee•cah•nah
mug	**la taza** lah tah•sah
postcard	**la postal** lah pohs•tahl
pottery	**la cerámica** lah seh•rah•mee•kah
T-shirt	**la playera** lah plah•yeh•rah
toy	**el juguete** ehl khoo•geh•teh
typical Mexican dress	**el vestido típico mexicano** ehl behs•tee•doh tee•pee•koh meh•khee•cah•noh
wine	**el vino** ehl bee•noh
Can I see *this/that*?	**¿Puedo ver *esto/eso*?** pweh•doh behr *ehs•toh/eh•soh*

It's in the *window/display case.*	**Está en *el aparador/la vitrina.*** ehs·tah ehn *ehl ah·pah·rah·dohr/lah bee·tree·nah*
I'd like...	**Quiero...** keeyeh·roh...
– a battery	**– una pila** oo·nah pee·lah
– a bracelet	**– una pulsera** oo·nah pool·seh·rah
– a brooch	**– un prendedor** oon prehn·deh·dohr
– earrings	**– unos aretes** oo·nohs ah·reh·tehs
– a necklace	**– un collar** oon koh·yahr
– a ring	**– un anillo** oon ah·nee·yoh
– a watch	**– un reloj de pulsera** oon rreh·lohkh deh pool·seh·rah
I'd like...	**Quiero...** keeyeh·roh...
– copper	**– cobre** koh·breh
– crystal	**– cristal** krees·tahl
– diamonds	**– diamantes** deeyah·mahn·tehs
– *white/yellow* gold	**– oro *blanco/amarillo*** oh·roh *blahn·koh/ah·mah·ree·yoh*
– pearls	**– perlas** pehr·lahs
– pewter	**– pewter** peh·oo·tehr
– platinum	**– platino** plah·tee·noh
– sterling silver	**– plata de ley** plah·tah deh lehee
Is this real?	**¿Es auténtico?** ehs awoo·tehn·tee·koh
Can you engrave it?	**¿Puede grabármelo?** pweh·deh grah·bahr·meh·loh

Mexico produces a wide range of souvenirs, from typical tourist T-shirts to high-quality regional crafts. Mexican tapestries and silverware are popular gifts. Specialty regional goods include copperware, pottery, leather goods, jewelry, lace, porcelain and wood carvings. To find a good sampling of the specialty goods in each Mexican town or city at reasonable prices, visit the **mercados de artesanías** (handicraft markets) in each town.

Throughout Mexico you can find quality gold and silver jewelry, especially in the famous southern city of Taxco. Jewelry can be purchased in jewelry stores, but for a more personal approach, visit the local markets. These, along with small specialty stores in rural villages and towns are a great source for handmade jewelry.

Antiques

How old is it?	**¿Qué antigüedad tiene?** keh ahn•tee•gweh•dahd teeyeh•neh
Do you have anything from the…period?	**¿Tiene algo de la época…?** teeyeh•neh ahl•goh deh lah eh•poh•kah…
Do I have to fill out any forms?	**¿Tengo que llenar algún formulario?** tehn•goh keh yeh•nahr ahl•goon fohr•moo•lah•reeoh
Is there a certificate of authenticity?	**¿Tiene el certificado de autenticidad?** teeyeh•neh ehl sehr•tee•fee•kah•doh deh awoo•tehn•tee•see•dahd

Clothing

I'd like…	**Quiero…** keeyeh•roh…
Can I try this on?	**¿Puedo probarme esto?** pweh•doh proh•bahr•meh ehs•toh
It doesn't fit.	**No me queda bien.** noh meh keh•dah beeyehn
It's too…	**Me queda demasiado…** meh keh•dah deh•mah•seeyah•doh…
– big	**– grande** grahn•deh
– small	**– chico**♂**/chica**♀ chee•koh♂/chee•kah♀
– short	**– corto**♂**/corta**♀ kohr•toh♂/kohr•tah♀
– long	**– largo**♂**/larga**♀ lahr•goh♂/lahr•gah♀

Do you have this in size…?	**¿Tiene esto en la talla…?** teeyeh·neh ehs·toh ehn lah tah·yah…
Do you have this in a *bigger/smaller* size?	**¿Tiene esto en una talla más *grande/chica*?** teeyeh·neh ehs·toh ehn oo·nah tah·yah mahs *grahn·deh/chee·kah*

▶For numbers, see page 178.

You May See…

ROPA DE CABALLERO	men's clothing
ROPA DE DAMA	women's clothing
ROPA DE NIÑOS	children's clothing

Color

I'd like something…	**Busco algo…** boos·koh ahl·goh…
– beige	**– beige** beh·eesh
– black	**– negro** neh·groh
– blue	**– azul** ah·sool
– brown	**– café** kah·feh
– green	**– verde** behr·deh
– gray	**– gris** grees
– orange	**– naranja** nah·rahn·khah
– pink	**– rosa** rroh·sah
– purple	**– morado** moh·rah·doh
– red	**– rojo** rroh·khoh
– white	**– blanco** blahn·koh
– yellow	**– amarillo** ah·mah·ree·yoh

Clothes and Accessories

backpack	**la mochila** lah moh·chee·lah
belt	**el cinturón** ehl seen·too·rohn
bikini	**el bikini** ehl bee·kee·nee
blouse	**la blusa** lah bloo·sah
bra	**el sostén** ehl sohs·tehn
briefs [underpants]	**los calzones** lohs kahl·sohn·nehs
coat	**el abrigo** ehl ah·bree·goh
dress	**el vestido** ehl behs·tee·doh
hat	**el sombrero** ehl sohm·breh·roh
jacket	**la chamarra** lah chah·mah·rrah
jeans	**los jeans** lohs jeens
pajamas	**la pijama** lah pee·khah·mah
pants [trousers]	**los pantalones** lohs pahn·tah·loh·nehs
pantyhose [tights]	**las medias** lahs meh·deeyahs
purse [handbag]	**la bolsa** lah bohl·sah
raincoat	**el impermeable** ehl eem·pehr·meh·ah·bleh
scarf	**la bufanda** lah boo·fahn·dah
shirt	**la camisa** lah kah·mee·sah
shorts	**los pantaloncillos** lohs pahn·tah·lohn·see·yohs
skirt	**la falda** lah fahl·dah
socks	**los calcetines** lohs kahl·seh·tee·nehs
suit	**el traje** ehl trah·kheh
sunglasses	**los lentes oscuros** lohs lehn·tehs ohs·koo·rohs
sweater	**el suéter** ehl sweh·tehr
sweatshirt	**la sudadera** lah soo·dah·deh·rah
swimsuit	**el traje de baño** ehl trah·kheh deh bah·nyoh

T-shirt	**la playera** lah plah·yeh·rah
tie	**la corbata** lah kohr·bah·tah
underwear	**la ropa interior** lah rroh·pah een·teh·reeyohr

Fabric

I'd like...	**Quiero...** keeyeh·roh...
– cotton	**– algodón** ahl·goh·dohn
– denim	**– mezclilla** mehs·klee·yah
– lace	**– encaje** ehn·kah·kheh
– leather	**– cuero** kweh·roh
– linen	**– lino** lee·noh
– silk	**– seda** seh·dah
– wool	**– lana** lah·nah
Is it machine washable?	**¿Se puede lavar en lavadora?** seh pweh·deh lah·bahr ehn lah·bah·doh·rah

Shoes

I'd like...	**Quiero...** keeyeh·roh...
– boots	**– botas** boh·tahs
– *high-heeled/flat* shoes	**– zapatos *de tacón/de piso*** sah·pah·tohs *deh tah·kohn/deh pee·soh*
– loafers	**– mocasines** moh·kah·see·nehs
– sandals	**– sandalias** sahn·dah·leeyahs
– shoes	**– zapatos** sah·pah·tohs
– slippers	**– pantuflas** pahn·too·flahs
– sneakers	**– tenis** teh·nees
In size...	**Tiene en número...** tee·eh·neh ehn noo·meh·roh...

▶For numbers, see page 178.

Sizes

small (S)	**pequeña (S)** peh•keh•nyah (eh•seh)
medium (M)	**mediana (M)** meh•deeyah•nah (eh•meh)
large (L)	**grande (L)** grahn•deh (eh•leh)
extra large (XL)	**extra grande** ehks•trah grahn deh
petite	**petite** peh•teet
plus size	**tallas extra** tah•yahs ehks•trah

Newsstand and Tobacconist

Do you sell English-language newspapers?	**¿Venden periódicos en inglés?** behn•dehn peh•reeyoh•dee•kohs ehn een•glehs
I'd like...	**Quiero...** keeyeh•roh...
– candy [sweets]	**– dulces** dool•sehs
– chewing gum	**– chicle** chee•kleh
– a chocolate bar	**– un chocolate** oon choh•koh•lah•teh
– a cigar	**– un puro** oon poo•roh
– a *pack/carton* of cigarettes	**– una *cajetilla/caja* de cigarros** oo•nah *kah•kheh•tee•yah/kah•khah* deh see•gah•rrohs
– a lighter	**– un encendedor** oon ehn•sehn•deh•dohr
– a magazine	**– una revista** oo•nah rreh•bees•tah
– matches	**– los cerillos** lohs seh•ree•yohs
– a newspaper	**– un periódico** oon peh•reeyoh•dee•koh
– a pen	**– una pluma** oo•nah ploo•mah
– a postcard	**– una postal** oo•nah pohs•tah
– a *road/town* map of...	**– un *mapa de las carreteras/plano* de...** oon *mah•pah deh lahs kah•rreh•teh•rahs/ plah•noh* deh...
– stamps	**– estampillas** ehs•tahm•pee•yahs

Photography

I'd like... camera.	**Quiero una cámara...** keeyeh·roh oo·nah kah·mah·rah...
– an automatic	**– automática** awoo·toh·mah·tee·kah
– a digital	**– digital** dee·khee·tahl
– a disposable	**– desechable** deh·seh·chah·bleh
I'd like...	**Quiero...** keeyeh·roh...
– a battery	**– una batería** oo·nah bah·teh·ree·ah
– digital prints	**– fotos digitales** foh·tohs dee·khee·tah·lehs
– a memory card	**– una tarjeta de memoria** oo·nah tahr·kheh·tah deh meh·moh·reeyah
Can I print digital photos here?	**¿Puedo imprimir aquí fotos digitales?** pweh·doh eem·pree·meer ah·kee foh·tohs dee·khee·tah·lehs

Sports and Leisure

Essential

When's the game?	**¿Cuándo empieza el partido?** kwahn·doh ehm·peeyeh·sah ehl pahr·tee·doh
Where's...?	**¿Dónde está...?** dohn·deh ehs·tah...
– the beach	**– la playa** lah plah·yah
– the park	**– el parque** ehl pahr·keh
– the pool	**– la alberca** lah ahl·behr·kah
Is it safe to swim here?	**¿Es seguro nadar aquí?** ehs seh·goo·roh nah·dahr ah·kee
Can I rent [hire] golf clubs?	**¿Puedo rentar palos de golf?** pweh·doh rrehn·tahr pah·lohs deh golf
How much per hour?	**¿Cuánto cuesta por hora?** kwahn·toh kwehs·tah pohr oh·rah

How far is it to...?	**¿A qué distancia está...?** ah keh dees•tahn•seeyah ehs•tah...
Can you show me on the map, please?	**¿Puede indicármelo en el mapa, por favor?** pweh•deh een•dee•kahr•meh•loh ehn ehl mah•pah pohr fah•bohr

Spectator Sports

When's...?	**¿Cuándo empieza...?** kwahn•doh ehm•peeyeh•sah...
– the basketball game	**– el partido de básquetbol** ehl pahr•tee•doh deh bahs•keht•bohl
– the boxing match	**– la pelea de box** lah peh•leh•ah deh bohx
– the cycling race	**– la carrera de bicicletas** lah kah•rreh•rah deh bee•see•kleh•tahs
– the golf tournament	**– el torneo de golf** ehl tohr•neh•oh deh golf
– the soccer [football] game	**– el partido de fútbol** ehl pahr•tee•doh deh foot•bohl
– the tennis match	**– el partido de tenis** ehl pahr•tee•doh deh teh•nees
– the volleyball game	**– el partido de voleibol** ehl pahr•tee•doh deh boh•lehee•bohl
Who's playing?	**¿Quiénes juegan?** keeyeh•nehs khweh•gahn
Where is...?	**¿Dónde está...?** dohn•deh ehs•tah...
– the horsetrack	**– el hipódromo** ehl ee•poh•droh•moh
– the racetrack	**– la pista de carreras** lah pees•tah de kah•rreh•rahs
– the stadium	**– el estadio** ehl ehs•tah•deeyoh
Where can I place a bet?	**¿Dónde puedo hacer una apuesta?** dohn•deh pweh•doh ah•sehr oo•nah ah•pwehs•tah

Fútbol (soccer) is the most popular sport in Mexico; most of the major cities in Mexico have their own professional teams with a large fan base. Note that fans are extremely dedicated, so be sure not to insult the team. Other popular sports include **fútbol americano** (American football), **básquetbol** (basketball), **boxeo** (boxing), **los toros** or **la fiesta brava** (bullfighting) and **lucha libre** (freestyle wrestling).

Though casinos are not legal in Mexico, one can gamble at the **hipódromo** (horsetrack), at **casas legales de apuestas** (legal betting houses) and at **tragamonedas** (electronic slot machines).

Participating

Where *is/are*...?	**¿Dónde *está/están*...?** dohn•deh *ehs•tah/ ehs•tahn*...
– the golf course	**– el campo de golf** ehl kahm•poh deh golf
– the gym	**– el gimnasio** ehl kheem•nah•seeyoh
– the park	**– el parque** ehl pahr•keh
– the tennis courts	**– las canchas de tenis** lahs kahn•chahs deh teh•nees

How much per…?	**¿Cuánto cuesta por…?** kwahn·toh kwehs·tah pohr…
– day	**– día** dee·ah
– hour	**– hora** oh·rah
– game	**– partido** pahr·tee·doh
– round	**– juego** khweh·goh
Can I rent [hire]…?	**¿Puedo rentar…?** pweh·doh rrehn·tahr…
– golf clubs	**– palos de golf** pah·lohs deh golf
– equipment	**– equipo** eh·kee·poh
– a racket	**– una raqueta** oo·nah rrah·keh·tah

At the Beach/Pool

Where's the *beach/pool*?	**¿Dónde está la *playa/alberca*?** dohn·deh ehs·tah lah *plah·yah/ahl·behr·kah*
Is there…?	**¿Hay…?** aye…
– a kiddie pool	**– un chapoteadero** oon chah·poh·teh·ah·deh·roh
– an *indoor/outdoor* pool	**– una alberca *cubierta/exterior*** oo·nah ahl·behr·kah *koo·beeyehr·tah/ehx·teh·reeyohr*
– a lifeguard	**– un salvavidas** oon sahl·bah·bee·dahs
Is it safe…?	**¿Es seguro…?** ehs seh·goo·roh…
– to swim	**– nadar** nah·dahr
– to dive	**– tirarse un clavado** tee·rahr·seh oon klah·bah·doh
– for children	**– para los niños** pah·rah lohs nee·nyohs

▶For travel with children, see page 155.

I'd like to rent [hire]...	**Quiero rentar...** keeyeh•roh rrehn•tahr...
– a deck chair	**– un camastro** oon kah•mahs•troh
– diving equipment	**– equipo de buceo** eh•kee•poh deh boo•seh•oh
– a jet ski	**– una moto acuática** oo•nah moh•toh ah•kwah•tee•kah
– a motorboat	**– una lancha de motor** oo•nah lahn•chah deh moh•tohr
– a rowboat	**– un bote de remos** oon boh•teh deh rreh•mohs
– snorkeling equipment	**– equipo de esnórquel** eh•kee•poh deh ehz•nohr•kehl
– a surfboard	**– una tabla de surf** oo•nah tah•blah deh soorf
– a towel	**– una toalla** oo•nah toh•ah•yah
– an umbrella	**– una sombrilla** oo•nah sohm•bree•yah
– water skis	**– unos esquís acuáticos** oo•nohs ehs•kees ah•kwah•tee•kohs
– a windsurfer	**– una tabla de windsurf** oo•nah tah•blah deh weend•soorf
For...hours.	**Por...horas.** pohr...oh•rahs

Mexico has many miles of coastline and beaches, boasting some of the most beautiful beaches in the Caribbean (Cancún, Cozumel, the Mayan Riviera) and the Pacific Coast (Huatulco, Ixtapa, Puerto Vallarta). If you decide to go for a swim, check the safety flags at each beach. Green flags indicate the water is safe, yellow flags indicate that you should use caution and red flags indicate that the water is unsafe for swimming.

Outdoor Sports

Where can I take kayak lessons?	**¿Dónde puedo tomar clases de kayak?** dohn•eeh pweh•doh toh•mahr clah•sehs deh kah•yahk
I'd like to rent [hire]...	**Quiero rentar...** keeyeh•roh rrehn•tahr...
– a bicycle	**– una bicicleta** oo•nah bee•see•cleh•tah
– boots	**– botas** boh•tahs
– climbing equipment	**– equipo de escalada** eh•kee•poh deh ehs•kah•lah•dah
– diving equipment	**– equipo de buceo** eh•kee•poh deh boo•seh•oh
– a helmet	**– un casco** oon kahs•koh
– a kayak	**– un kayak** oon kah•yahk
These are too *big/small.*	**Me quedan demasiado *grandes/chicos.*** meh keh•dahn deh•mah•seeyah•doh *grahn•dehs/chee•kohs*
Are there lessons?	**¿Dan clases?** dahn klah•sehs
I'm a beginner.	**Soy principiante.** soy preen•see•peeyahn•teh
I'm experienced.	**Tengo experiencia.** tehn•goh ehx•peh•reeyehn•seeyah
A trail [piste] map, please.	**Un mapa de las pistas, por favor.** oon mah•pah deh lahs pees•tahs pohr fah•bohr

Mexico has no shortage of great outdoor sports. Its privileged location and biodiversity make Mexico a great place for recreation. You can explore it by train, horse or bicycle, on foot or by kayak, camping or climbing mountains.

However, when embarking on any outdoor activity, make sure to hire a local guide who is an expert in the activity as well as on the location.

You May See...

CICLÍSMO	cycling
ESCALADA	climbing
BUCEO	diving
PRINCIPIANTE	novice
NIVEL INTERMEDIO	intermediate
EXPERTO	expert
PISTA CERRADA	trail [piste] closed

In the Countryside

A map of…, please.	**Un mapa de…, por favor.** oon mah·pah deh…pohr fah·bohr
– the bike routes	**– las rutas para bicicletas** lahs rroo·tahs pah·rah bee·see·kleh·tahs
– the trails	**– los senderos** lohs sehn·deh·rohs
– the walking routes	**– las rutas de caminata** lahs rroo·tahs deh kah·mee·nah·tah
– this region	**– esta región** ehs·tah rreh·kheeyohn
Is it *easy/difficult*?	**¿Es *fácil/difícil*?** ehs *fah·seel/dee·fee·seel*
Is it *far/steep*?	**¿Está *lejos/con pendiente*?** ehs·tah *leh·khohs/kohn pehn·deeyehn·teh*
How far is it to…?	**¿A qué distancia está…?** ah keh dees·tahn·seeyah ehs·tah…
Can you show me on the map, please?	**¿Puede indicármelo en el mapa, por favor?** pweh·deh een·dee·kahr·meh·loh ehn ehl mah·pah pohr fah·bohr
I'm lost.	**Me perdí.** meh pehr·dee

Where is...?	**¿Dónde está...?** dohn·deh ehs·tah...
– the bridge	– **el puente** ehl pwehn·teh
– the cave	– **la cueva** lah kweh·bah
– the cliff	– **el acantilado** ehl ah·kahn·tee·lah·doh
– the desert	– **el desierto** ehl deh·seeyehr·toh
– the farm	– **la granja** lah grahn·khah
– the field	– **el campo** ehl kahm·poh
– the forest	– **el bosque** ehl bohs·keh
– the hill	– **el cerro** ehl seh·rroh
– the lake	– **el lago** ehl lah·goh
– the mountain	– **la montaña** lah mohn·tah·nyah
– the nature preserve	– **la reserva natural** lah rreh·sehr·bah nah·too·rahl
– the overlook [viewpoint]	– **el mirador** ehl mee·rah·dohr
– the park	– **el parque** ehl pahr·keh
– the path	– **el camino** ehl kah·mee·noh
– the peak	– **el pico** ehl pee·koh
– the picnic area	– **el área para día de campo** ehl ah·reh·ah pah·rah dee·ah deh kahm·poh
– the pond	– **el estanque** ehl ehs·tahn·keh
– the river	– **el río** ehl rree·oh
– the sea	– **el mar** ehl mahr
– the (thermal) spring	– **el manantial (de aguas termales)** ehl mah·nahn·teeyahl (deh ah·gwahs tehr·mah·lehs)
– the stream	– **el arroyo** ehl ah·rroh·yoh
– the valley	– **el valle** ehl bah·yeh
– the vineyard	– **el viñedo** ehl bee·nyeh·doh
– the waterfall	– **la cascada** lah kahs·kah·dah

Culture and Nightlife

Essential

What's there to do at night?	**¿Qué se puede hacer en la noche?** keh seh pweh·deh ah·sehr ehn lah noh·cheh
Do you have a program of events?	**¿Tiene un programa de eventos?** teeyeh·neh oon proh·grah·mah deh eh·behn·tohs
What's playing tonight?	**¿Qué hay en cartelera esta noche?** keh aye ehn kahr·teh·leh·rah ehs·tah noh·cheh
Where's...?	**¿Dónde está...?** dohn·deh ehs·tah...
– the downtown area	**– el centro** ehl sehn·troh
– the bar	**– el bar** ehl bahr
– the dance club	**– la discoteca** lah dees·koh·teh·kah
Is there a cover charge?	**¿Hay que pagar cover?** aye keh pah·gahr koh·behr

Mexican culture today is the result of the rise and fall of its numerous Amerindian civilizations combined with 300 years of Spanish rule. This eclecticism is clearly visible in Mexican art. Folk art, such as pottery, carvings or metal work, is extremely popular and pieces are available for viewing in museums and for purchase throughout the country. You can also see Mexican tradition reflected in the works of the many modern Mexican painters such as the famous muralists, José Clemente Orozco, Diego Rivera and David Alfaro Siqueiros, or Rufino Tamayo and Frida Kahlo. In Mexico City, exhibitions by these artists are on display in the Bellas Artes Museum, the Modern Art Museum or the Carrillo Gil Museum; both Rivera and Tamayo have their own museums as well.

Entertainment

Can you recommend...?	**¿Puede recomendarme...?** pweh·deh rreh·koh·mehn·dahr·meh...
– a concert	**– un concierto** oon kohn·seeyehr·toh
– a movie	**– una película** oo·nah peh·lee·koo·lah
– an opera	**– una ópera** oo·nah oh·peh·rah
– a play	**– una obra de teatro** oo·nah oh·brah deh teh·ah·troh
When does it *start/end*?	**¿A qué hora *empieza/termina*?** ah keh oh·rah *ehm·peeyeh·sah/tehr·mee·nah*
What's the dress code?	**¿Cómo hay que ir vestido ♂/vestida ♀?** koh·moh aye keh eer behs·tee·doh ♂/ behs·tee·dah ♀
I like...	**Me gusta...** meh goos·tah...
– classical music	**– la música clásica** lah moo·see·kah klah·see·kah
– folk music	**– la música folclórica** lah moo·see·kah fohl·kloh·ree·kah
– jazz	**– el jazz** ehl jahzz
– pop music	**– la música pop** lah moo·see·kah pop
– rap	**– el rap** ehl rrahp

▶For ticketing, see page 20.

You May Hear...

Por favor apaguen sus celulares. pohr fah·bohr ah·pah·gehn soos sehl·yoo·lah·rehs	Turn off your cell [mobile] phones, please.

i Mexico is a vast country with no shortage of entertainment options. For a taste of traditional Mexican entertainment, you could attend a dance performance. Two popular styles include **mopolka**, a dance representing a man honoring a woman, and **metachine**, a dance performed on special holidays by soldiers wearing masks. A music performance is another entertainment option. Traditional options include: **banda**, brass-based music originally with a strong Native American influence; **corridos**, ballads; **norteño**, a style originating from the North; **ranchera**, which originated on Mexican ranches; as well as **mariachis**, traditional musical groups.

Nightlife

What's there to do at night?	**¿Qué se puede hacer en la noche?** keh seh pweh•deh ah•sehr ehn lah noh•cheh
Can you recommend...?	**¿Puede recomendarme...?** pweh•deh rreh•koh•mehn•dahr•meh...
– a bar	**– un bar** oon bahr
– a bingo hall	**– un bingo** oon been•goh
– a club with traditional Mexican music	**– un bar con música típica mexicana** oon bahr kohn moo•see•kah tee•pee•kah me meh•khee•kah•nah
– a dance club	**– una discoteca** oo•nah dees•koh•teh•kah
– a gay club	**– una discoteca gay** oo•nah dees•koh•teh•kah gay
– a mariachi performance	**– un espectáculo de mariachis** oon ehs•pehk•tah•koo•loh deh mah•ree•ah•chees
– a jazz club	**– un club de jazz** oon kloob deh jazz
Is there live music?	**¿Hay música en vivo?** aye moo•see•kah ehn bee•boh
How do I get there?	**¿Cómo llego allí?** koh•moh yeh•goh ah•yee

Is there a cover charge?	**¿Hay que pagar cover?** aye keh pah•gahr koh•behr
Let's go dancing.	**Vamos a bailar.** bah•mohs ah bayee•lahr

The **mariachi** is a type of musical group, originally from Cocula, Jalisco. Usually a **mariachi** (also known as **los mariachis**) band consists of violins, trumpets, guitars, **vihuela** (a high-pitched, five string guitar) and **guitarrón** (an acoustic bass). Professional **mariachis** are normally singers skilled at playing more than one instrument. Trios or larger groups of **mariachis** (up to 12 band members) can be found for hire for serenading women; the best known venues are Plaza de los Mariachis in Guadalajara and Plaza Garibaldi in downtown Mexico City. They are also hired to liven up various celebrations.

▼ Special Needs

Business Travel

Essential

I'm here on business. **Estoy aquí en viaje de negocios.** ehs·toy ah·kee ehn beeyah·kheh deh neh·goh·seeyohs

Here's my business card. **Aquí tiene mi tarjeta.** ah·kee teeyeh·neh mee tahr·kheh·tah

Can I have your card? **¿Puede darme su tarjeta?** pweh·deh dahr·meh soo tahr·kheh·tah

I have a meeting with… **Tengo una reunión con…** tehn·goh oo·nah rrewoo·neeyohn kohn…

Where's…? **¿Dónde está…?** dohn·deh ehs·tah…

– the business center **– el centro de negocios** ehl sehn·troh deh neh·goh·seeyohs

– the convention hall **– el salón de congresos** ehl sah·lohn deh kohn·greh·sohs

– the meeting room **– la sala de reuniones** lah sah·lah deh rrewoo·neeyohn·ehs

Business Communication

I'm here to attend… **Estoy aquí para asistir…** ehs·toy ah·kee pah·rah ah·sees·teer…

– a seminar **– a un seminario** ah oon seh·mee·nah·reeyoh

– a conference **– a una conferencia** ah oo·nah kohn·feh·rehn·seeyah

– a meeting **– a una reunión** ah oo·nah rrewoo·neeyohn

My name is… **Me llamo…** meh yah·moh…

I have *a meeting/an appointment* with… **Tengo una *reunión/cita* con…** tehn·goh oo·nah *rrewoo·neeyohn/see·tah* kohn…

May I introduce my colleague...	**Le presento a mi compañero ♂ / compañera ♀ de trabajo...** leh preh·sehn·toh ah mee kohm·pah·nyeh·roh ♂ / kohm·pah·nyeh·rah ♀ deh trah·bah·khoh...
I'm sorry I'm late.	**Disculpe que haya llegado tarde.** dees·kool·peh keh ah·yah yeh·gah·doh tahr·deh
I need an interpreter.	**Necesito un intérprete.** neh·seh·see·toh oon een·tehr·preh·teh
You can reach me at the...Hotel.	**Puede encontrarme en el Hotel...** pweh·deh ehn·kohn·trahr·meh ehn ehl oh·tehl...
I'm here until...	**Estaré aquí hasta...** ehs·tah·reh ah·kee ahs·tah...
I need to...	**Necesito...** neh·seh·see·toh...
– make a call	**– hacer una llamada** ah·sehr oo·nah yah·mah·dah
– make a photocopy	**– sacar una fotocopia** sah·kahr oo·nah foh·toh·koh·peeyah
– send an e-mail	**– enviar un correo electrónico** ehn·bee·ahr oon koh·rreh·oh ee·lehk·troh·nee·koh

I need to…	**Necesito…** neh•seh•see•toh…
– send a fax	**– enviar un fax** ehn•bee•ahr oon fahx
– send a package (overnight)	**– enviar un paquete (para entrega el día siguiente)** ehn•bee•ahr oon pah•keh•teh (pah•rah ehn•treh•gah ehl dee•ah see•geeyehn•teh)
It is a pleasure to meet you.	**Mucho gusto.** moo•choh goos•toh

▶For internet and communications, see page 50.

It is common to greet colleagues with **buenos días** (good morning). Shake hands if it is the first time you are meeting someone in a professional setting, or if it is someone you haven't seen in a while. When leaving, simply say **adiós**, **gracias** or **hasta luego** (goodbye, thank you or see you later).

You May Hear…

¿Tiene cita? teeyeh•neh see•tah	Do you have an appointment?
¿Con quién? kohn keeyehn	With whom?
Está en una reunión. ehs•tah ehn oo•nah rrewoo•neeyohn	He/She is in a meeting.
Un momento, por favor. oon moh•mehn•toh pohr fah•bohr	One moment, please.
Siéntese. seeyehn•teh•seh	Have a seat.
¿Quiere algo de tomar? keeyeh•reh ahl•goh deh toh•mahr	Would you like something to drink?
Gracias por su visita. grah•seeyahs pohr soo bee•see•tah	Thank you for coming.

Travel with Children

Essential

Is there a discount for kids?	**¿Hacen descuento para niños?** ah·sen dehs·kwehn·toh pah·rah nee·nyohs
Can you recommend a babysitter?	**¿Puede recomendarme una niñera?** pweh·deh rreh·koh·mehn·dahr·meh oo·nah neeh·nyeh·rah
Do you have a *child's seat/ highchair*?	**¿Tienen una *silla para niños/periquera*?** teeyeh·nehn oo·nah *see·yah pah·rah nee·nyohs/peh·ree·keh·rah*
Where can I change the baby?	**¿Dónde puedo cambiar al bebé?** dohn·deh pweh·doh kahm·beeyahr ahl beh·beh

Fun with Kids

Can you recommend something for kids?	**¿Puede recomendarme algo para los niños?** pweh·deh rreh·koh·mehn·dahr·meh ahl·goh pah·rah lohs nee·nyohs
Where's...?	**¿Dónde está...?** dohn·deh ehs·tah...
– the amusement park	**– el parque de diversiones** ehl pahr·keh deh dee·behr·seeyoh·nehs
– the arcade	**– la sala de juegos** lah sah·lah deh khweh·gohs
– the kiddie [paddling] pool	**– el chapoteadero** ehl chah·poh·teh·ah·deh·roh
– the park	**– el parque** ehl pahr·keh
– the playground	**– el parque infantil** ehl pahr·keh een·fahn·teel
– the zoo	**– el zoológico** ehl soh·oh·loh·khee·koh
Are kids allowed?	**¿Se permite la entrada a niños?** seh pehr·mee·teh lah ehn·trah·dah ah nee·nyohs

Is it safe for kids?	**¿Es seguro para niños?** ehs seh•goo•roh pah•rah nee•nyohs
Is it suitable for... year olds?	**¿Es adecuado para niños de.. años?** ehs ah•deh•koo•ah•doh pah•rah nee•nyohs deh... ah•nyohs

▶For numbers, see page 178.

You May Hear...

¡Qué bonito♂/bonita♀! keh boh•nee•toh ♂/ boh•nee•tah ♀	How cute!
¿Cómo se llama? koh•moh seh yah•mah	What's his/her name?
¿Qué edad tiene? keh eh•dahd teeyeh•neh	How old is he/she?

Basic Needs for Kids

Do you have...?	**¿Tiene...?** teeyeh•neh...
– a baby bottle	**– un biberón** oon bee•beh•rohn
– baby wipes	**– toallitas** toh•ah•yee•tahs
– a car seat	**– un asiento para niños** oon ah•seeyehn•toh pah•rah nee•nyohs

– a children's *menu/portion*	– ***un menú/una ración* para niños** *oon meh-noo/oo-nah rrah-seeyohn* pah-rah nee-nyohs
– a *child's seat/ highchair*	– **una *silla para niños/periquera*** oo-nah *see-yah pah-rah nee-nyohs/peh-ree-khe-rah*
– a *crib/cot*	– **una cuna/un catre** oo-nah koo-nah/oon kah-treh
– diapers [nappies]	– **pañales** pah-nyah-lehs
– formula	– **fórmula** fohr-moo-lah
– a pacifier [soother]	– **un chupón** oon choo-pohn
– a playpen	– **un corral** oon koh-rrahl
– a stroller [pushchair]	– **una carriola** oo-nah kah-rreeyoh-lah
Can I breastfeed the baby here?	**¿Puedo darle pecho al bebé aquí?** pweh-doh dahr-leh peh-choh ahl beh-beh ah-kee
Where can I change the baby?	**¿Dónde puedo cambiar al bebé?** dohn-deh pweh-doh kahm-beeyahr ahl beh-beh

▶For dining with kids, see page 65.

Babysitting

Can you recommend a babysitter?	**¿Puede recomendarme una niñera?** pweh-deh rreh-koh-mehn-dahr-meh oo-nah neeh-nyeh-rah
What's the charge?	**¿Cuánto cuesta?** kwahn-toh kwehs-tah
I'll be back by…	**Vuelvo a la/las…** bwehl-boh ah lah/lahs…
I can be reached at…	**Puede encontrarme en el…** pweh-deh ehn-kohn-trahr-meh ehn ehl…

▶For when to use **la** or **las**, see page 174.

▶For time, see page 180.

Health and Emergency

Can you recommend a pediatrician?	**¿Puede recomendarme un pediatra?** pweh•deh rreh•koh•mehn•dahr•meh oon peh•deeyah•trah
My *son/daughter* is allergic to...	**Mi *hijo/hija* es alérgico♂/alérgica♀ a...** mee *ee•khoh/ee•khah* ehs ah•lehr•khee•koh♂/ ah•lehr•khee•kah♀ ah
My *son/daughter* is missing.	**Mi *hijo/hija* ha desaparecido.** mee *ee•khoh/ee•khah* ah deh•sah•pah•reh•see•doh
Have you seen a *boy/girl*?	**¿Ha visto a *un niño/una niña*?** ah bees•toh ah oon nee•nyoh/oo•nah nee•nyah

▶For food items, see page 90.
▶For health, see page 163.

For the Disabled

Essential

Is there...?	**¿Hay...?** aye...
– access for the disabled	**– acceso para los discapacitados** ahk•seh•soh pah•rah lohs dees•kah•pah•see•tah•dohs
– a wheelchair ramp	**– una rampa para sillas de ruedas** oo•nah rrahm•pah pah•rah see•yahs deh rrweh•dahs
– a handicapped-[disabled-] accessible toilet	**– un baño con acceso para discapacitados** oon bah•nyoh kohn ahk•seh•soh pah•rah dees•kah•pah•see•tah•dohs
I need...	**Necesito...** neh•seh•see•toh...
– assistance	**– ayuda** ah•yoo•dah
– an elevator [a lift]	**– un elevador** oon eh•leh•bah•dohr
– a ground-floor room	**– una habitación en la planta baja** oo•nah ah•bee•tah•seeyohn ehn lah plahn•tah bah•khah

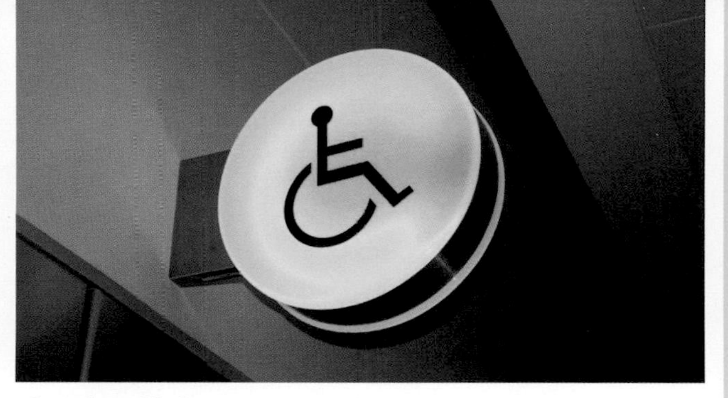

Getting Help

I'm disabled.	**Soy discapacitado ♂/discapacitada ♀.** soy dees•kah•pah•see•tah•doh ♂/ dees•kah•pah•see•tah•dah ♀
I'm deaf.	**Soy sordo ♂/sorda ♀.** soy sohr•doh ♂/ sohr•dah ♀
I'm *visually/hearing* impaired.	**Tengo discapacidad *visual/auditiva.*** tehn•goh dees•kah•pah•see•dahd *bee•swahl/ awoo•dee•tee•bah*
I'm unable to *walk far/use the stairs.*	**No puedo *caminar muy lejos/subir las escaleras.*** noh pweh•doh *kah•mee•nahr mooyee leh•khohs/soo•beer lahs ehs•kah•leh•rahs*
Can I bring my wheelchair?	**¿Puedo traer la silla de ruedas?** pweh•doh trah•ehr lah see•yah deh rrweh•dahs
Are guide dogs permitted?	**¿Permiten a perros guía?** pehr•mee•tehn ah peh•rrohs gee•ah
Can you help me?	**¿Puede ayudarme?** pweh•deh ah•yoo•dahr•meh
Please *open/hold* the door.	**Por favor, *abra/sostenga* la puerta.** pohr fah•bohr *ah•brah/sohs•tehn•gah* lah pwehr•tah

▼ Resources

Emergencies

Essential

Help!	**¡Auxilio!** aw•xee•leeyoh
Go away!	**¡Váyase!** bah•yah•seh
Stop, thief!	**¡Alto, ladrón!** ahl•toh lah•drohn
Get a doctor!	**¡Llame a un doctor!** yah•meh ah oon dohk•tohr
Fire!	**¡Fuego!** fweh•goh
I'm lost.	**Me perdí.** meh pehr•dee
Can you help me?	**¿Puede ayudarme?** pweh•deh ah•yoo•dahr•meh

Police

Essential

Call the police!	**¡Llame a la policía!** yah•meh ah lah poh•lee•see•ah
Where's the police station?	**¿Dónde está la estación de policia?** dohn•deh ehs•tah lah ehs•tah•seeyohn deh poh•lee•see•ah
There was an *accident/attack*.	**Hubo un *accidente/asalto*.** ooh•boh oon *ahk•see•dehn•teh/ah•sahl•toh*
My *son/daughter* is missing.	**Mi *hijo/hija* desapareció.** mee *ee•khoh/ee•khah* deh•sah•pah•reh•seeyoh
I need…	**Necesito…** neh•seh•see•toh…
– an interpreter	**– un intérprete** oon een•tehr•preh•teh
– to contact my lawyer	**– ponerme en contacto con mi abogado** poh•nehr•meh ehn kohn•tahk•toh kohn mee ah•boh•gah•doh

I need…	**Necesito…** neh•seh•see•toh…
– to make a phone call	**– hacer una llamada** ah•sehr oo•nah yah•mah•dah
I'm innocent.	**Soy inocente.** soy ee•noh•sehn•teh

You May Hear…

Llene este formulario. yeh•neh ehs•teh fohr•mooh•lah•reeoh	Fill out this form.
Su identificación, por favor. soo ee•dehn•tee•fee•kah•seeyohn pohr fah•bohr	Your identification, please
¿*Cuándo/Dónde* ocurrió? *kwahn•doh/ dohn•deh* oh•koo•rreeyoh	*When/Where* did it happen?
¿Puede describirlo♂/describirla♀? pweh•deh dehs•kree•beer•loh♂/ dehs•kree•beer•lah♀	What does he/she look like?

Lost Property and Theft

I'd like to report…	**Quiero denunciar…** keeyeh•roh deh•noon•seeyahr…
– a mugging	**– una agresión** oo•nah ah•greh•seeyohn
– a rape	**– una violación** oo•nah beeyoh•lah•seeyohn
– a theft	**– un robo** oon rroh•boh
I was *mugged/ robbed.*	**Me *asaltaron/atracaron.*** meh *ah•sahl•tah•rohn/ah•trah•kah•rohn*
I lost my…	**Perdí mi…** pehr•dee mee…
My… *was/were* stolen.	**Me robaron…** meh rroh•bah•rohn…
– backpack	**– la mochila** lah moh•chee•lah
– bicycle	**– la bicicleta** lah bee•see•kleh•tah

– camera	**– la cámara** lah kah•mah•rah
– (rental [hire]) car	**– el auto rentado** ehl awoo•toh (rrehn•tah•doh)
– computer	**– la computadora** lah kohm•poo•tah•doh•rah
– credit card	**– la tarjeta de crédito** lah tahr•kheh•tah deh kreh•dee•toh
– jewelry	**– las joyas** lahs khoh•yahs
– money	**– el dinero** ehl dee•neh•roh
– passport	**– el pasaporte** ehl pah•sah•pohr•teh
– purse [handbag]	**– el bolso** ehl bohl•soh
– traveler's checks [cheques]	**– los cheques de viajero** lohs cheh•kehs deh beeyah•kheh•roh
– wallet	**– la cartera** lah kahr•teh•rah
I need a police report.	**Necesito un acta ministerial.** neh•seh•see•toh oon ahk•tah mee•nees•teh•reeyahl

Health

Essential

I'm sick [ill].	**Me siento mal.** meh seeyehn•toh mahl
I need an English-speaking doctor.	**Necesito un doctor que hable inglés.** neh•seh•see•toh oon dohk•tohr keh ah•bleh een•glehs
It hurts here.	**Me duele aquí.** meh dweh•leh ah•kee
I have a stomachache.	**Tengo dolor de estómago.** tehn•goh doh•lohr deh ehs•toh•mah•goh

Finding a Doctor

Can you recommend a *doctor/dentist*?	**¿Puede recomendarme un *doctor/dentista*?** pweh·deh rreh·koh·mehn·dahr·meh oon *dohk·tohr/dehn·tees·tah*
Can the doctor come here?	**¿Podría el doctor venir aquí?** poh·dree·ah ehl dohk·tohr beh·neer ah·kee
I need an English-speaking doctor.	**Necesito un doctor que hable inglés.** neh·seh·see·toh oon dohk·tohr keh ah·bleh een·glehs
What are the office hours?	**¿Cuáles son las horas de consulta?** kwah·lehs sohn lahs oh·rahs deh kohn·sool·tah
I'd like an appointment...	**Quiero una cita...** keeyeh·roh oo·nah see·tah...
– for today	**– para hoy** pah·rah oy
– for tomorrow	**– para mañana** pah·rah mah·nyah·nah
– as soon as possible	**– lo antes posible** loh ahn·tehs poh·see·bleh
It's urgent.	**Es urgente.** ehs oor·khehn·teh

Symptoms

I'm...	**Estoy...** ehs·toy...
– bleeding	**– sangrando** sahn·grahn·doh
– constipated	**– estreñido♂/estreñida♀** ehs·treh·nyee·doh♂/ ehs·treh·nyee·dah♀
– dizzy	**– mareado♂/mareada♀** mah·reh·ah·doh♂/ mah·reh·ah·dah♀
I'm *nauseous/vomiting.*	**Tengo *náuseas/vómitos.*** tehn·goh *naw·seh·ahs/boh·mee·tohs*
It hurts here.	**Me duele aquí.** meh dweh·leh ah·kee
I have...	**Tengo...** tehn·goh...
– an allergic reaction	**– una reacción alérgica** oo·nah rreh·ahk·seeyohn ah·lehr·khee·kah

– chest pain	**– dolor de pecho** doh•lohr deh peh•choh
– an earache	**– dolor de oído** doh•lohr deh oh•ee•doh
– a fever	**– fiebre** feeyeh•breh
– pain	**– dolor** doh•lohr
– a rash	**– un salpullido** oon sahl•poo•yee•doh
– a sprain	**– un esguince** oon ehz•geen•seh
– some swelling	**– una hinchazón** oo•nah een•chah•sohn
– a stomachache	**– dolor de estómago** doh•lohr deh ehs•toh•mah•goh
– sunstroke	**– una insolación** oo•nah een•soh•lah•seeyohn
I've been sick [ill] for...days.	**Hace...días que me siento mal.** ah•seh...dee•ahs keh meh seeh•ehn•toh mahl

▶For numbers, see page 178.

Health Conditions

I'm...	**Soy...** soy...
– anemic	**– anémico♂/anémica♀** ah•neh•mee•koh♂/ ah•neh•mee•kah♀
– asthmatic	**– asmático♂/asmática♀** ahz•mah•tee•koh♂/ahz•mah•tee•kah♀
– diabetic	**– diabético♂/diabética♀** deeyah•beh•tee•koh♂/deeyah•beh•tee•kah♀
I'm allergic to *antibiotics/penicillin.*	**Soy alérgico♂/alérgica♀ a *los antibióticos/la penicilina.*** soy ah•lehr•khee•koh♂/ah•lehr•khee•kah♀ ah *lohs ahn•tee•beeyoh•tee•kohs/lah peh•nee•see•lee•nah*

▶For food items, see page 90.

I have...	**Tengo...** tehn•goh...
– arthritis	**– artritis** ahr•tree•tees
– high blood pressure	**– la presión alta** lah preh•seeyohn ahl•tah
– low blood pressure	**– la presión baja** lah preh•seeyohn bah•khah
I have a heart condition.	**Padezco del corazón.** pah•dehs•koh dehl koh•rah•son
I'm on...	**Estoy tomando...** ehs•toy toh•mahn•doh...

Hospital

Notify my family, please.	**Por favor, avise a mi familia.** pohr fah•bohr ah•bee•seh ah mee fah•mee•leeyah
I'm in pain.	**Tengo dolor.** tehn•goh doh•lohr
I need a *doctor/nurse.*	**Necesito *un doctor/una enfermera.*** neh•seh•see•toh *oon dohk•tohr/oo•nah ehn•fehr•meh•rah*
When are visiting hours?	**¿Cuál es el horario de visitas?** kwal ehs ehl oh•rah•ree•oh deh bee•see•tahs
I'm visiting...	**Vengo a hacer una visita a...** behn•goh ah ah•sehr oo•nah bee•see•tah ah...

You May Hear...

¿Qué le pasa? keh leh pah•sah	What's wrong?
¿Dónde le duele? dohn•deh leh dweh•leh	Where does it hurt?
¿Le duele aquí? leh dweh•leh ah•kee	Does it hurt here?
¿Está tomando algún medicamento? ehs•tah toh•mahn•doh ahl•goon meh•dee•kah•mehn•toh	Are you on medication?
¿Es alérgico♂/alérgica♀ a algo? ehs ah•lehr•khee•koh♂/ah•lehr•khee•kah♀ ah ahl•goh	Are you allergic to anything?
Abra la boca. ah•brah lah boh•kah	Open your mouth.
Respire hondo. rrehs•pee•reh ohn•doh	Breathe deeply.
Tiene que ir al hospital. teeyeh•neh keh eer ahl ohs•pee•tahl	Go to the hospital.

Dentist

I've *broken a tooth/lost a filling.*	**Se me *rompió un diente/cayó una tapadura.*** seh meh *rrohm•peeyoh oon deeyehn•teh/kah•yoh oo•nah tah•pah•doo•rah*
I have a toothache.	**Tengo dolor de muelas.** tehn•goh doh•lohr deh mweh•lahs
Can you fix this denture?	**¿Puede arreglarme la dentadura postiza?** pweh•deh ah•rreh•glahr•meh lah dehn•tah•doo•rah pohs•tee•sah

Gynecologist

I have *menstrual cramps/a vaginal infection.* — **Tengo *dolores menstruales/una infección vaginal.*** tehn·goh *doh·loh·rehs mehns·trwah·lehs/oo·nah een·fehk·seeyohn bah·khee·nahl*

I missed my period. — **No me ha bajado la regla.** noh meh ah bah·khah·doh lah rreh·glah

I'm on the Pill. — **Tomo anticonceptivos.** toh·moh ahn·tee·kohn·sehp·tee·bohs

I'm (not) pregnant. — **(No) Estoy embarazada.** (noh) ehs·toy ehm·bah·rah·sah·dah

My last period was... — **La última vez que me bajó la regla fue...** lah ool·tee·mah behs keh meh bah·khoh lah rreh·glah fweh...

Optician

I lost... — **Perdí...** pehr·dee...

– a contact lens — **– un lente de contacto** oon lehn·teh deh kohn·tahk·toh

– my glasses — **– los anteojos** lohs ahn·teh·oh·khohs

– a lens — **– una lente** oo·nah lehn·teh

Payment and Insurance

How much? — **¿Cuánto es?** kwahn·toh ehs

Can I pay by credit card? — **¿Puedo pagar con tarjeta de crédito?** pweh·doh pah·gahr kohn tahr·kheh·tah deh kreh·dee·toh

I have insurance. — **Tengo seguro médico.** tehn·goh seh·goo·roh meh·dee·koh

I need a receipt for my insurance. — **Necesito una factura para el seguro médico.** neh·seh·see·toh oo·nah fahk·too·rah pah·rah ehl seh·goo·roh meh·dee·koh

Pharmacy [Chemist]

Essential

Where's the pharmacy [chemist]?	**¿Dónde está la farmacia?** dohn•deh ehs•tah lah fahr•mah•seeyah
What time does it *open/close*?	**¿A qué hora *abre/cierra*?** ah keh oh•rah *ah•breh/seeyeh•rrah*
What would you recommend for…?	**¿Qué me recomienda para…?** keh meh rreh•koh•meeyehn•dah pah•rah…
How much do I take?	**¿Qué dosis tomo?** keh doh•sees toh•moh
Can you fill [make up] this prescription?	**¿Puede darme este medicamento?** pweh•deh dahr•meh ehs•teh meh•dee•kah•mehn•toh
I'm allergic to…	**Soy alérgico♂/alérgica♀ a…** soy ah•lehr•khee•koh♂/ah•lehr•khee•kah♀ ah…

There is a wide variety of pharmacies in Mexico, including generic drugstores which sell unbranded medication only. Most drugstores offer a variety of toiletries and other goods, in addition to dispensing medicines. Business hours are usually from 9:00 a.m. until 7:00 p.m. In smaller towns, pharmacies may close during lunch time. There are 24-hour pharmacies available in larger cities.

Dosage Instructions

How much do I take?	**¿Qué dosis tomo?** keh doh·sees toh·moh
How often?	**¿Con qué frecuencia?** kohn keh freh·kwehn·seeyah
Is it safe for children?	**¿Es adecuado para niños?** ehs ah·deh·kwah·doh pah·rah nee·nyohs
I'm taking…	**Estoy tomando…** ehs·toy toh·mahn·doh…
Are there side effects?	**¿Tiene algún efecto secundario?** teeyeh·neh ahl·goon eh·fehk·toh seh·koon·dah reeyoh

You May See…

***UNA VEZ/TRES VECES* AL DÍA**	*once/three* times a day
COMPRIMIDO	tablet
GOTA	drop
CUCHARADITA	teaspoon
***DESPUÉS DE/ANTES DE/CON* LAS COMIDAS**	*after/before/with* meals
CON EL ESTÓMAGO VACÍO	on an empty stomach
TRAGUE EL COMPRIMIDO ENTERO	swallow whole
PUEDE CAUSAR SUEÑO	may cause drowsiness
DE USO TÓPICO SOLAMENTE	for external use only

Health Problems

I need something for…	**Necesito algo para…** neh·seh·see·toh ahl·goh pah·rah…
– a cold	**– el resfrío** ehl rrehs·free·oh
– a cough	**– la tos** lah tohs

– diarrhea	– **la diarrea** lah deeyah·rreh·ah
– insect bites	– **las picaduras de insecto** lahs pee·kah·doo·rahs deh een·sehk·toh
– motion [travel] sickness	– **el mareo** ehl mah·reh·oh
– a sore throat	– **las anginas** lahs ahn·khee·nahs
– sunburn	– **las quemaduras del sol** lahs keh·mah·doo·rahs deh sohl
– an upset stomach	– **el malestar estomacal** ehl mah·lehs·tahr ehs·toh·mah·kahl

Basic Needs

I'd like...	**Quiero...** keeyeh·roh...
– acetaminophen [paracetamol]	– **paracetamol** pah·rah·seh·tah·mohl
– antiseptic cream	– **pomada antiséptica** poh·mah·dah ahn·tee·sehp·tee·kah
– aspirin	– **aspirinas** ahs·pee·ree·nahs
– bandages	– **curitas** koo·ree·tahs
– a comb	– **un peine** oon peyee·neh
– condoms	– **condones** kohn·doh·nehs
– contact lens solution	– **líquido para lentes de contacto** lee·kee·doh pah·rah lehn·tehs deh kohn·tahk·toh
– deodorant	– **desodorante** deh·soh·doh·rahn·teh
– a hairbrush	– **un cepillo para el pelo** oon seh·pee·yoh pah·rah ehl peh·loh
– ibuprofen	– **ibuprofeno** ee·boo·proh·feh·noh
– insect repellent	– **repelente de insectos** rreh·peh·lehn·teh deh een·sehk·tohs
– lotion	– **crema hidratante** kreh·mah ee·drah·tahn·teh

I'd like…	**Quiero…** keeyeh·roh…
– a razor	**– una navaja de afeitar** oo·nah nah·bah·khah deh ah·fehee·tahr
– razor blades	**– hojas de afeitar** oh·khahs deh ah·feyee·tahr
– sanitary napkins [pads]	**– toallas sanitarias** toh·ah·yas sah·nee·tah·reeyahs
– shampoo/ conditioner	**– champú/acondicionador** chahm·poo/ ah·kohn·dee·seeyoh·nah·dohr
– soap	**– jabón** khah·bohn
– sunscreen	**– protector solar** proh·tehk·tohr soh·lahr
– tampons	**– tampones** tahm·poh·nehs
– tissues	**– pañuelos desechables** pah·nyweh·lohs deh·seh·chah·blehs
– toilet paper	**– papel higiénico** pah·pehl ee·kheeyeh·nee·koh
– a toothbrush	**– un cepillo de dientes** oon seh·pee·yoh deh deeyehn·tehs
– toothpaste	**– pasta de dientes** pahs·tah deh deeyehn·tehs

▶For basic needs for kids, see page 156.

Grammar

In Spanish, there are a number of forms for "you" (taking different verb forms): **tú** (singular) is informal, and used when talking to relatives, close friends and children; **usted** (singular) is used in all other cases and the plural **ustedes** is both formal and informal. If in doubt, use **usted** for "you". The following abbreviations are used in this section: **Ud.** = **Usted**; **Uds.** = **Ustedes**; sing. = singular; pl. = plural; inf. = informal; for. = formal.

Regular Verbs

There are three verb types that follow a regular conjugation pattern. These verbs end in **–ar**, **–er** and **–ir**. Following are the present, past and future forms of the verbs **hablar** (to speak), **comer** (to eat) and **vivir** (to live). The different conjugation endings are in bold.

HABLAR		Present	Past	Future
I	**yo**	habl**o**	habl**é**	habl**aré**
you (sing.)	**tú**	habl**as**	habl**aste**	habl**arás**
he/she/ you (for.)	**él/ella/Ud.**	habl**a**	habl**ó**	habl**ará**
we	**nosotros**	habl**amos**	habl**amos**	habl**aremos**
they/you (pl.)	**ellos♂/ellas♀/ Uds.**	habl**an**	habl**aron**	habl**arán**

COMER		Present	Past	Future
I	**yo**	com**o**	com**í**	com**eré**
you (sing.)	**tú**	com**es**	com**iste**	com**erás**
he/she/ you (for.)	**él/ella/Ud.**	com**e**	com**ió**	com**erá**
we	**nosotros**	com**emos**	com**imos**	com**eremos**
they/you (pl.)	**ellos♂/ellas♀/ Uds.**	com**en**	com**ieron**	com**erán**

VIVIR		Present	Past	Future
I	**yo**	viv**o**	viv**í**	viv**iré**
you (sing.)	**tú**	viv**es**	viv**iste**	viv**irás**
he/she/ you (for.)	**él/ella/Ud.**	viv**e**	viv**ió**	viv**irá**
we	**nosotros**	viv**imos**	viv**imos**	viv**iremos**
they/you (pl.)	**ellos♂/ellas♀/ Uds.**	viv**en**	viv**ieron**	viv**irán**

Irregular Verbs

In Spanish, there are many different irregular verbs; these aren't conjugated by following the normal rules. The two most commonly used, and confused, irregular verbs are **ser** and **estar**. Both verbs mean "to be". Following is the past, present and future tenses of **ser** and **estar** for easy reference.

SER	Present	Past	Future
yo	soy	fui	seré
tú	eres	fuiste	serás
él/ella/Ud.	es	fue	será
nosotros	somos	fuimos	seremos
ellos/ellas/Uds.	son	fueron	serán

ESTAR	Present	Past	Future
yo	estoy	estuve	estaré
tú	estás	estuviste	estarás
él/ella/Ud.	está	estuvo	estará
nosotros	estamos	estuvimos	estaremos
ellos/ellas/Uds.	están	estuvieron	estarán

Ser is used to describe a fixed quality or characteristic. It is also used to tell time and dates.

Example: **Yo soy estadounidense.** I am American.

Here **ser** is used because it is a permanent characteristic.

Estar is used when describing a physical location or a temporary condition.

Example: **Estoy cansado.** I am tired.

Here **estar** is used because being tired is a temporary condition.

Nouns and Articles

Nouns are either masculine or feminine. Masculine nouns usually end in **–o**, and feminine nouns usually end in **–a**. Nouns become plural by adding an **–s**, or **–es** to nouns not ending in **–o** or **–a** (e.g. **tren** becomes **trenes**).

Nouns in Spanish take an indefinite (a, an or some) or definite (the) article. An article must agree with the noun to which it refers in gender and number.

Indefinite examples: **un tren** ♂ (a train); **unos trenes** ♂ (some trains); **una mesa** ♀ (a table); **unas mesas** ♀ (some tables)

Definite examples: **el libro** ♂ (the book); **los libros** ♂ (the books); **la casa** ♀ (the house); **las casas** ♀ (the houses)

Word Order

In Spanish, the conjugated verb comes after the subject.

Example: **Yo trabajo en Guadalajara.** I work in Guadalajara.

To ask a question, reverse the order of the subject and verb, change your intonation or use key question words such as **cuándo** (when).

Examples: **¿Cuándo cierra el banco?** When does the bank close?

Literally translates to: "When closes the bank?" Notice the order of the subject and verb is reversed; a question word also begins the sentence.

¿El hotel es viejo? Is the hotel old?

Literally: The hotel is old? This is a statement that becomes a question by raising the pitch of the last syllable of the sentence.

Negation

To form a negative sentence, add **no** (not) before the verb.

Example: **Fumamos.** We smoke.

No fumamos. We don't smoke.

Imperatives

Imperative sentences, or sentences that are commands, are formed by adding the appropriate ending to the stem of the verb (i.e. the verb in the infinitive without the **-ar**, **-er**, **-ir** ending). Example: Speak!

you (sing.) (inf.)	**tú**	**¡Habla!**
you (sing.) (for.)	**Ud.**	**¡Hable!**
we	**nosotros**	**¡Hablemos**
you (pl.) (for.)	**Uds.**	**¡Hablen!**

Comparative and Superlative

The comparative is usually formed by adding **más** (more) or **menos** (less) before the adjective or noun. The superlative is formed by adding the appropriate definite article (**la/las**, **el/los**) and **más** (the most) or **menos** (the least) before the adjective or noun. Example:

grande	**más grande**	**el♂/la♀ más grande**
big	bigger	biggest
caro♂/cara♀	**menos caro♂/cara♀**	**el♂/la♀ menos caro♂/cara♀**
expensive	less expensive	least expensive

Possessive Pronouns

Pronouns serve as substitutes for specific nouns and must agree with the noun in gender and number.

	Singular	Plural
mine	**mío♂/mía♀**	**míos♂/mías♀**
yours (inf.)	**tuyo♂/tuya♀**	**tuyos♂/tuyas♀**
yours (for.)	**suyo♂/suya♀**	**suyos♂/suyas♀**
his/her/its	**suyo♂/suya♀**	**suyos♂/suyas♀**
ours	**nuestro♂/nuestra♀**	**nuestros♂/nuestras♀**
theirs	**suyo♂/suya♀**	**suyos♂/suyas♀**

Example: **Ese asiento es mío.** That seat is mine.

Possessive Adjectives

A possessive adjective must agree in number and gender with the noun that follows.

	Singular	Plural
my	**mi**	**mis**
your (inf.)	**tu**	**tus**
his/her/its	**su**	**sus**
our	**nuestro**♂/**nuestra**♀	**nuestros**♂/**nuestras**♀
their/your (for.)	**su**	**sus**

Examples: **¿Dónde está su chamarra?** Where is your jacket?

Tu vuelo sale a las ocho. Your flight leaves at eight.

Adjectives

Adjectives describe nouns and must agree with the noun in gender and number. In Spanish, adjectives usually come after the noun. Masculine adjectives generally end in **–o**, feminine adjectives in **–a**. If the masculine form ends in **–e** or with a consonant, the feminine form is generally the same. Most adjectives form their plurals the same way as nouns.

Example: **Su *hijo/hija* es simpático**♂/**simpática**♀. Your *son/ daughter* is nice.

Adverbs and Adverbial Expressions

Some adverbs are formed by adding **–mente** to the adjective.

Example: **Roberto conduce lentamente.** Robert drives slowly.

The following are some common adverbial time expressions:

actualmente presently

todavía no not yet

todavía still

ya no not anymore

Numbers

Essential

0	**cero** seh·roh
1	**uno** oo·noh
2	**dos** dohs
3	**tres** trehs
4	**cuatro** kwah·troh
5	**cinco** seen·koh
6	**seis** seyees
7	**siete** seeyeh·teh
8	**ocho** oh·choh
9	**nueve** nweh·beh
10	**diez** deeyehs
11	**once** ohn·seh
12	**doce** doh·seh
13	**trece** treh·seh
14	**catorce** kah·tohr·seh
15	**quince** keen·seh
16	**dieciséis** deeyeh·see·seyees
17	**diecisiete** deeyeh·see·seeyeh·teh
18	**dieciocho** deeyeh·see·oh·choh
19	**diecinueve** deeyeh·see·nweh·beh
20	**veinte** beyeen·teh
21	**veintiuno** beyeen·tee·oo·noh
22	**veintidós** beyeen·tee·dohs
30	**treinta** treyeen·tah

31	**treinta y uno** treyeen·tah ee oo·noh
40	**cuarenta** kwah·rehn·tah
50	**cincuenta** seen·kwehn·tah
60	**sesenta** seh·sehn·tah
70	**setenta** seh·tehn·tah
80	**ochenta** oh·chehn·tah
90	**noventa** noh·behn·tah
100	**cien** seeyehn
101	**ciento uno** seeyehn·toh oo·noh
200	**doscientos** dohs·seeyehn·tohs
500	**quinientos** kee·neeyehn·tohs
1,000	**mil** meel
10,000	**diez mil** deeyehs meel
1,000,000	**un millón** oon mee·yohn

Ordinal Numbers

first	**primero ♂ /primera ♀** pree·meh·roh ♂ /pree·meh·rah ♀
second	**segundo ♂ /segunda ♀** seh·goon·doh ♂ /seh·goon·dah ♀
third	**tercero ♂ /tercera ♀** tehr·seh·roh ♂ /tehr·seh·rah ♀
fourth	**cuarto ♂ /cuarta ♀** kwahr·toh ♂ /kwahr·tah ♀
fifth	**quinto ♂ /quinta ♀** keen·toh ♂ /keen·tah ♀
once	**una vez** oo·nah behs
twice	**dos veces** dohs beh·ses
three times	**tres veces** trehs beh·ses

Essential

What time is it? **¿Qué hora es?** keh oh·rah ehs

It's noon [midday]. **Son las doce del día.** sohn lahs doh·seh dehl dee·ah

At midnight. **A medianoche.** ah meh·deeyah·noh·cheh

From one o'clock to two o'clock. **De una a dos en punto.** deh oo·nah ah dohs ehn poon·toh

Five after three. **Las tres y cinco.** lahs trehs ee seen·koh

A quarter to five. **Cuarto para las cinco.** kwahr·toh pah·rah lahs seen·koh

5:30 *a.m./p.m.* **Las cinco y media de la *mañana/tarde*.** lahs seen·koh ee meh·deeyah deh lah *mah·nyah·nah/tahr·deh*

In Mexico the 24-hour clock is used when writing time, especially in schedules. The morning hours from 1:00 a.m. to noon are the same as in English. After that, just add 12 to the time: 1:00 p.m. would be 13:00, 5:00 p.m. would be 17:00 and so on.

Days

Essential

Monday	**lunes** loo·nehs
Tuesday	**martes** mahr·tehs
Wednesday	**miércoles** meeyehr·koh·lehs
Thursday	**jueves** khweh·behs
Friday	**viernes** beeyehr·nehs
Saturday	**sábado** sah·bah·doh
Sunday	**domingo** doh·meen·goh

Dates

yesterday	**ayer** ah·yehr
today	**hoy** oy
tomorrow	**mañana** mah·nyah·nah
day	**día** dee·ah
week	**semana** seh·mah·nah
month	**mes** mehs
year	**año** ah·nyoh

Months

January	**enero** eh·neh·roh
February	**febrero** feh·breh·roh
March	**marzo** mahr·soh
April	**abril** ah·breel
May	**mayo** mah·yoh
June	**junio** khoo·neeyoh
July	**julio** khoo·leeyoh

August **agosto** ah·gohs·toh
September **septiembre** sehp·teeyehm·breh
October **octubre** ohk·too·breh
November **noviembre** noh·beeyehm·breh
December **diciembre** dee·seeyehm·breh

Mexico follows a day-month-year format:
Examples: el uno de marzo de 2009 = March 1, 2009
1.3.09 = 3/1/2009

Seasons

spring **la primavera** lah pree·mah·beh·rah
summer **el verano** ehl beh·rah·noh
fall [autumn] **el otoño** ehl oh·toh·nyoh
winter **el invierno** ehl een·beeyehr·noh

Holidays

January 1: New Year's Day, **Año Nuevo**

February 5: Constitution Day, **Día de la Constitución**

March 21: Benito Juarez Day, **Natalicio de Benito Juarez**

May 1: Labor Day, **Día del Trabajo**

May 5: Battle of Puebla, **Día de la Batalla de Puebla** (non official holliday)

September 16: Mexico's Independence Day, **Día de la Independencia**

November 2: All Saint's Day, **Fieles Difuntos**

November 20: Mexican Revolution's Day, **Día de la Revolución Mexicana**

December 12: Feast of the Virgin of Guadalupe, **Día de la Virgen de Guadalupe**

December 25: Christmas, **Navidad**

Moveable Holiday

Easter: **Pascua**

Conversion Tables

When you know	Multiply by	To find
ounces	28.3	grams
pounds	0.45	kilograms
inches	2.54	centimeters
feet	0.3	meters
miles	1.61	kilometers
square inches	6.45	sq. centimeters
square feet	0.09	sq. meters
square miles	2.59	sq. kilometers
pints (U.S./Brit)	0.47/0.56	liters
gallons (U.S./Brit)	3.8/4.5	liters
Fahrenheit	5/9, after –32	Centigrade
Centigrade	9/5, then +32	Fahrenheit

Mileage

1 km – 0.62 mi	20 km – 12.4 mi
5 km – 3.10 mi	50 km – 31.0 mi
10 km – 6.20 mi	100 km – 61.0 mi

Measurement

1 gram	**un gramo** oon grah•moh	= 0.035 oz.
1 kilogram (kg)	**un kilogramo** oon kee•loh•grah•moh	= 2.2 lb
1 liter (l)	**un litro** oon lee•troh	= 1.06 U.S./0.88 Brit. quarts
1 centimeter (cm)	**un centímetro** oon sehn•tee•meh•troh	= 0.4 inch
1 meter (m)	**un metro** oon meh•troh	= 3.28 ft.
1 kilometer (km)	**un kilómetro** oon kee•loh•meh•troh	= 0.62 mile

Temperature

-40° C – -40° F	-1° C – 30° F	20° C – 68° F
-30° C – -22° F	0° C – 32° F	25° C – 77° F
-20° C – -4° F	5° C – 41° F	30° C – 86° F
-10° C – 14° F	10° C – 50° F	35° C – 95° F
-5° C – 23° F	15° C – 59° F	

Oven Temperature

100° C – 212° F	177° C – 350° F
121° C – 250° F	204° C – 400° F
149° C – 300° F	260° C – 500° F

Useful Websites

www.visitmexico.com
Official Tourism Board of Mexico site

www.sectur.gob.mx
Official website of the Mexico Secretariat of Tourism

www.mexicocity.gob.mx
Official website of Mexico City Secretariat of Tourism

www.df.gob.mx
Official website of Mexico City

www.metro.df.gob.mx
Mexico City subway information

www.aeromexico.com
Aeromexico's website

www.asociaciondehoteles.com.mx
Mexico City's Hotel Association

www.amr.org.mx
Mexican Association of Restaurants

www.hotelesmexicanos.org
Mexican Association of Hotels and Motels

www.amtave.com
Mexican Association of Adventure, Tourism and Ecotourism

www.sepomex.gob.mx
Official post office website of Mexico

www.descubrebajacalifornia.com/ruta_vino/index.html
Vineyard tours website

www.hihostels.com
Hostelling International site

www.berlitzpublishing.com
Berlitz phrase books and travel guides

English–Spanish Dictionary

A

abbey la abadía
accept *v* aceptar
access el acceso
accident el accidente
accommodation el alojamiento
account la cuenta
acupuncture la acupuntura
adapter el adaptador
address la dirección
admission la entrada
after después; **~noon** la tarde; **~shave** la loción para después de afeitar
age la edad
agency la agencia
AIDS el sida
air el aire; **~ conditioning** el aire acondicionado; **~line** la aerolínea; **~mail** el correo aéreo; **~plane** el avión; **~port** el aeropuerto
aisle el pasillo; **~ seat** el asiento de pasillo
allergic alérgico; **~ reaction** la reacción alérgica
allow *v* permitir
alone solo
alter *v* **(clothing)** hacer un ajuste
alternate route el otro camino
aluminum foil el papel aluminio
amazing increíble
ambulance la ambulancia
American estadounidense
amusement park el parque de diversiones
anemic anémico
anesthesia la anestesia
animal el animal
ankle el tobillo
antibiotic el antibiótico
antiques store la tienda de antigüedades
antiseptic cream la pomada antiséptica
anything algo
apartment el departamento
appendix (body part) el apéndice
appetizer el aperitivo
appointment la cita
arcade el salón de juegos de video
area code el código de área
arm el brazo
aromatherapy la aromaterapia
around (the corner) doblando (la esquina)
arrivals (airport) las llegadas
arrive *v* llegar
artery la arteria
arthritis la artritis
arts las letras
aspirin la aspirina
asthmatic asmático
ATM el cajero automático
attack la agresión
attend *v* asistir

adj	adjective	**BE**	British English	**v**	verb
adv	adverb	**n**	noun		

attraction (place) el sitio de interés
attractive guapo
Australia Australia
Australian australiano
automatic automático; **~ car** auto automático
available disponible

B

baby el bebé; **~ bottle** el biberón; **~ wipe** la toallita; **~sitter** la niñera
back la espalda; **~ache** el dolor de espalda; **~pack** la mochila
bag la maleta
baggage el equipaje; **~ claim** el reclamo de equipaje; **~ ticket** el talón de equipaje
bakery la panadería
ballet el ballet
bandage la curita
bank el banco
bar el antro
barbecue la parrillada
barber la peluquería
baseball el béisbol
basket (grocery store) la canasta
basketball el básquetbol
bathroom el baño
battery la pila
battery (car) la batería
battleground el campo de batalla
be *v* ser/estar
beach la playa
beautiful bello
bed la cama; **~ and breakfast** la pensión
before antes de
begin *v* empezar
beginner principiante
behind detrás de
beige beige
belt el cinturón
berth la litera
best mejor
better mejor
bicycle la bicicleta
big grande
bigger más grande
bike route la ruta para bicicletas
bikini el bikini; **~ wax** la depilación de las ingles
bill *v* **(charge)** cobrar; **~** *n* **(money)** el billete; **~** *n* **(of sale)** el recibo
bird el pájaro
birthday el cumpleaños
black negro
bladder la vejiga
bland insípido
blanket la cobija
bleed *v* sangrar
blood la sangre; **~ pressure** la presión arterial
blouse la blusa
board *v* embarcar
boarding pass el pase de abordar
boat el barco
bone el hueso
book el libro; **~store** la librería
boots las botas
boring aburrido
botanical garden el jardín botánico
bother *v* molestar
bottle la botella; **~ opener** el destapador
bowl el tazón
box la caja

boxing match la pelea de boxeo
boy el niño; **~friend** el novio
bra el sostén
bracelet la pulsera
brakes (car) los frenos
break *v* romper
break-in (burglary) el allanamiento de morada
breakdown la avería
breakfast el desayuno
breast el seno; **~feed** dar pecho
breathe *v* respirar
bridge el puente
briefs (clothing) los calzones
bring *v* traer
British británico
broken roto
brooch el broche
broom la escoba
brother el hermano
bug el insecto
building el edificio
burn *v* quemar
bus el camión; **~ station** la estación de camiones; **~ stop** la parada de camiones; **~ ticket** el boleto del camión; **~ tour** el recorrido en camión
business los negocios; **~ card** la tarjeta de presentación; **~ center** el centro de negocios; **~ class** la clase ejecutiva; **~ hours** el horario de atención al público
butcher el carnicero
buttocks los gluteos
buy *v* comprar
bye adiós

C

cabin (house) la cabaña; **~ (ship)** el camarote
cable car el teleférico
cafe la cafetería
call *v* llamar; **~** *n* la llamada
calories las calorías
camera la cámara; **~ case** el estuche para la cámara; **~ store** la tienda de fotografía; **digital ~** la cámara digital
camp *v* acampar; **~site** el campamento
can opener el abrelatas
Canada Canadá
Canadian canadiense
cancel *v* cancelar
candy el caramelo
canned goods las conservas
canyon el cañón
car el auto; **~ hire [BE]** la renta de autos; **~ park [BE]** el estacionamiento; **~ rental** el alquiler de autos; **~ seat** el asiento de niño
carafe la jarra
card la tarjeta; **ATM ~** la tarjeta de cajero automático; **credit ~** la tarjeta de crédito; **debit ~** la tarjeta de débito; **phone ~** la tarjeta de teléfono
carry-on (piece of hand luggage) el equipaje de mano
cart (grocery store) el carrito; **~ (luggage)** el carrito para el equipaje
carton el cartón; **~ of cigarettes** la cajetilla de cigarros
case (amount) la caja

cash *v* cobrar; **~** *n* el efectivo; **~ advance** sacar dinero de la tarjeta
cashier el cajero
castle el castillo
cathedral la catedral
cave la cueva
CD el CD
cell phone el teléfono celular
Celsius el grado centígrado
centimeter el centímetro
certificate el certificado
chair la silla
change *v* **(buses)** transbordar; **~** *n* **(money)** el cambio
charcoal el carbón
charge *v* **(credit card)** cobrar; **~** *n* **(cost)** el precio
cheap barato
check *v* **(on something)** revisar; **~** *v* **(luggage)** registrar; **~** *n* **(payment)** el cheque; **~-in (airport)** la documentación; **~-in (hotel)** el registro; **~ing account** la cuenta corriente; **~-out (hotel)** la salida
Cheers! ¡Salud!
chemical toilet el excusado químico
chemist [BE] la farmacia
cheque [BE] el cheque
chest (body part) el pecho; **~ pain** el dolor de pecho
chewing gum el chicle
child el niño; **~ seat** la silla para niños
children's menu el menú para niños
children's portion la ración para niños
church la iglesia
cigar el puro
cigarette el cigarrillo
class la clase; **business ~** la clase ejecutiva; **economy ~** la clase turista; **first ~** la primera clase
classical music la música clásica
clean *v* limpiar; **~** *adj* limpio; **~ing product** el producto de limpieza; **~ing supplies** los productos de limpieza
clear *v* **(on an ATM)** borrar
cliff el acantilado
cling film [BE] el plástico transparente
close *v* **(a shop)** cerrar
closed cerrado
clothing la ropa; **~ store** la tienda de ropa
club la discoteca
coat el abrigo
coffee shop la cafetería
coin la moneda
colander el colador
cold *n* **(sickness)** el resfriado; **~** *adj* **(temperature)** frío
colleague el compañero de trabajo
cologne la colonia
color el color
comb el peine
come *v* venir
complaint la queja
computer la computadora
concert el concierto; **~ hall** la sala de conciertos
condition (medical) el problema de salud
conditioner el acondicionador
condom el condón
conference la conferencia
confirm *v* confirmar

congestion la congestión
connect *v* **(internet)** conectarse
connection (internet) la conexión; **~ (flight)** la conexión de vuelo
constipated estreñido
consulate el consulado
consultant el consultor
contact *v* ponerse en contacto con
contact lens el lente de contacto; **~ solution** el líquido para lentes de contacto
contagious contagioso
convention hall el centro de congresos
conveyor belt la cinta transportadora
cook *v* cocinar
cooking gas el gas butano
cool (temperature) frío
copper el cobre
corkscrew el sacacorchos
cost *v* costar
cot el catre
cotton el algodón
cough *v* toser; **~** *n* la tos
country code el código de país
cover charge el cover
crash *v* **(car)** estrellarse
cream (ointment) la pomada
credit card la tarjeta de crédito
crew neck el cuello redondo
crib la cuna
crystal el cristal
cup la taza
currency la moneda; **~ exchange** el cambio de divisas; **~ exchange office** la casa de cambio
current account [BE] la cuenta de cheques
customs las aduanas
cut *v* **(hair)** cortar; **~** *n* **(injury)** el corte
cute bonito
cycling el ciclismo

D

damage *v* causar daño
damaged ha sufrido daños
dance *v* bailar; **~ club** la discoteca
dangerous peligroso
dark oscuro
date (calendar) la fecha
day el día
deaf sordo
debit card la tarjeta de débito
deck chair el camastro
declare *v* declarar
decline *v* **(credit card)** rechazar
deep hondo
degrees (temperature) los grados
delay *v* retrasar
delete *v* **(computer)** borrar
delicatessen la salchichonería
delicious delicioso
denim la mezclilla
dentist el dentista
denture la dentadura
deodorant el desodorante
department store las tiendas departamentales
departures (airport) las salidas
deposit *v* depositar; **~** *n* **(bank)** el depósito bancario; **~** *n* **(reserve a room)** el depósito
desert el desierto
dessert el postre

detergent el detergente
develop *v* **(film)** revelar
diabetic diabético
dial *v* marcar
diamond el diamante
diaper el pañal
diarrhea la diarrea
diesel el diésel
difficult difícil
digital digital; **~ camera** la cámara digital; **~ photos** las fotos digitales; **~ prints** las fotos digitales
dining room el comedor
dinner la cena
direction la dirección
dirty sucio
disabled discapacitado
disconnect (computer) desconectar
discount el descuento
dish (kitchen) el plato; **~washer** el lavaplatos; **~washing liquid** el líquido lavaplatos
display *v* mostrar; **~ case** la vitrina
disposable desechable; **~ razor** la cuchilla desechable
dive *v* bucear
diving equipment el equipo de buceo
divorce *v* divorciar
dizzy mareado
doctor el doctor
doll la muñeca
dollar (U.S.) el dólar
domestic nacional; **~ flight** el vuelo nacional
door la puerta
dormitory el dormitorio
double bed la cama matrimonial
downtown el centro
dozen la docena
dress (piece of clothing) el vestido; **~ code** las normas de vestimenta
drink *v* beber; **~** *n* la bebida; **~ menu** la carta de bebidas; **~ing water** el agua potable
drive *v* conducir
driver's license number licencia de conducir
drop (medicine) la gota
drowsiness la somnolencia
dry cleaner la tintorería
dubbed doblado
during durante
duty (tax) el impuesto; **~-free** libre de impuestos
DVD el DVD

E

ear la oreja; **~ache** el dolor de oído
early temprano
earrings los aretes
east el este
easy fácil
eat *v* comer
economy class la clase turista
elbow el codo
electric outlet el enchufe
elevator el elevador
e-mail *v* enviar un correo electrónico; **~** *n* el correo electrónico; **~ address** la dirección de correo electrónico

emergency la urgencia;
~ exit la salida de emergencia
empty *v* vaciar
enamel (jewelry) el esmalte
end *v* terminar
English el inglés
engrave *v* grabar
enjoy *v* disfrutar
enter *v* entrar
entertainment el entretenimiento
entrance la entrada
envelope el sobre
equipment el equipo
escalators las escaleras eléctricas
e-ticket el boleto electrónico
evening la noche
excess el exceso
exchange *v* **(money)** cambiar;
~ *v* **(goods)** devolver;
~ *n* **(place)** la casa de cambio;
~ rate el tipo de cambio
excursion la excursión
excuse *v* **(to get past)** pedir perdón; **~** *v* **(to get attention)** disculparse
exhausted agotado
exit *v* salir; **~** *n* la salida
expensive caro
expert (skill level) experto
exposure (film) la foto
express rápido; **~ bus** el camión rápido; **~ train** el tren rápido
extension (phone) la extensión
extra adicional; **~ large** extra grande
extract *v* **(tooth)** extraer
eye el ojo
eyebrow wax la depilación de cejas

F

face la cara
facial el facial
family la familia
fan (appliance) el ventilador;
~ (souvenir) el abanico
far lejos; **~-sighted** hipermétrope
farm la granja
fast rápido; **~ food** la comida rápida
father el padre
fax *v* enviar un fax; **~** *n* el fax;
~ number el número de fax
fee la tarifa
feed *v* alimentar
ferry el transbordador
fever la fiebre
field (sports) la cancha
fill *v* llenar ; **~ out** *v* **(form)** llenar
filling (tooth) la tapadura
film (camera) el rollo
fine (fee for breaking law) la multa
finger el dedo; **~nail** la uña
fire fuego; **~ department** los bomberos; **~ door** la puerta de incendios
first primero; **~ class** la primera clase
fit (clothing) quedar bien
fitting room el probador
fix *v* **(repair)** reparar
flashlight la linterna
flight el vuelo
floor el suelo
flower la flor
folk music la música folclórica
food la comida
foot el pie

football [BE] el fútbol
for para/por
forecast el pronóstico
forest el bosque
fork el tenedor
form el formulario
formula (baby) la fórmula
fort el fuerte
fountain la fuente
free gratuito
freezer el congelador
fresh fresco
friend el amigo
frying pan el sartén
full completo;**~-service** el servicio completo; **~-time** de tiempo completo

G

game el partido
garage (parking) el garaje; **~ (repair)** el taller
garbage bag la bolsa de basura
gas la gasolina; **~ station** la gasolinera
gate (airport) la puerta
gay gay; **~ bar** el antro gay; **~ club** la discoteca gay
gel (hair) el gel
get off *v* **(a train/bus/subway)** bajarse
get to *v* ir a
gift el regalo; **~ shop** la tienda de regalos
girl la niña; **~friend** la novia
give *v* dar
glass (drinking) el vaso; **~ (material)** el vidrio
glasses los anteojos
go *v* **(somewhere)** ir a
gold el oro
golf golf; **~ course** el campo de golf; **~ tournament** el torneo de golf
good *n* el producto; **~** *adj* bueno; **~ afternoon** buenas tardes; **~ evening** buenas noches; **~ morning** buenos días; **~bye** adiós
gram el gramo
grandchild el nieto
grandparents los abuelos
grocery store el supermercado
ground la tierra; **~ floor** la planta baja; **~cloth** la tela impermeable
group el grupo
guide el guía; **~ book** la guía; **~ dog** el perro guía
gym el gimnasio
gynecologist el ginecólogo

H

hair el pelo; **~ dryer** el secador de pelo; **~ salon** el salón de belleza; **~ stylist** el estilista; **~brush** el cepillo de pelo; **~cut** el corte de pelo; **~spray** la laca; **~style** el peinado
half medio; **~ hour** la media hora; **~-kilo** el medio kilo
hammer el martillo
hand la mano; **~ luggage [BE]** el equipaje de mano **~bag [BE]** el bolso;
handicapped discapacitado
hangover la cruda
happy feliz
hat el sombrero
have *v* tener

head (body part) la cabeza; **~ache** el dolor de cabeza; **~phones** los audífonos
health la salud; **~ food store** la tienda de alimentos naturales
heart el corazón; **~ condition** padecer del corazón
heat *v* calentar; **~***n* el calor
heater la calefacción
hello hola
helmet el casco
help *v* ayudar; **~***n* la ayuda
here aquí
hi hola
high alto; **~ chair** la periquera; **~way** la autopista
hiking boots las botas de excursionista
hill la colina
hire *v* **[BE]** alquilar; **~ car [BE]** el coche de alquiler
hitchhike pedir aventón
hockey el hockey
holiday [BE] las vacaciones
horse track el hipódromo
hospital el hospital
hostel el hostal
hot (temperature) caliente; **~ (spicy)** picante; **~ spring** el agua termal; **~ water** el agua caliente
hotel el hotel
hour la hora
house la casa; **~hold goods** los artículos para el hogar; **~keeping services** el servicio de limpieza de habitaciones
how (question) cómo; **~ much (question)** cuánto cuesta
hug *v* abrazar
hungry hambriento
hurt *v* **(have pain)** tener dolor
husband el esposo

I

ibuprofen el ibuprofeno
ice el hielo; **~ hockey** el hockey sobre hielo
icy helado
identification la identificación
ill *v* **(to feel)** sentirse mal
in dentro
include *v* incluir
indoor pool la alberca cubierta
inexpensive barato
infected infectado
information (phone) el número de teléfono de información; **~ desk** el módulo de información
insect el insecto; **~ bite** el piquete de insecto; **~ repellent** el repelente de insectos
insert *v* introducir
insomnia el insomnio
instant message el mensaje instantáneo
insulin la insulina
insurance el seguro; **~ card** la credencial de seguro; **~company** la compañía de seguros
interesting interesante
intermediate el nivel intermedio
international (airport area) internacional; **~ flight** el vuelo internacional; **~ student card** la credencial internacional de

estudiante
internet el Internet; ~ **cafe** el café Internet; ~ **service** el servicio de Internet; **wireless** ~ el acceso inalámbrico
interpreter intérprete
intersection el cruce
intestine el intestino
introduce *v* presentar
invoice [BE] la factura
Ireland Irlanda
Irish irlandés
iron *n* la plancha; ~ *v* **(clothes)** planchar

J

jacket la chamarra
jar el bote
jaw la mandíbula
jazz el jazz; ~ **club** el club de jazz
jeans los jeans
jet ski la moto acuática
jeweler's la joyería
jewelry las joyas
join *v* acompañar a
joint (body part) la articulación

K

key la llave; ~ **card** la llave electrónica; ~ **ring** el llavero
kiddie pool el chapoteadero
kidney (body part) el riñón
kilo el kilo; **~gram** el kilogramo; **~meter** el kilómetro
kiss *v* besar
kitchen la cocina; ~ **foil [BE]** el papel aluminio
knee la rodilla
knife el cuchillo

L

lace el encaje
lactose intolerant intolerante a la lactosa
lake el lago
large grande
last último
late (time) tarde
laundrette [BE] la lavandería
laundromat la lavandería
laundry lavar ropa; ~ **service** el servicio de lavandería
lawyer el abogado
leather el cuero
to leave *v* salir
left (direction) la izquierda
leg la pierna
lens el lente
less menos
lesson la lección
letter la carta
library la biblioteca
life la vida; ~ **jacket** el chaleco salvavidas; **~guard** rescatista
lift *n* **[BE]** el elevador; ~ *v* **(to give a ride)** llevar en auto; ~ **pass** el pase de acceso a los remontes
light *n* **(overhead)** la luz; ~ *v* **(cigarette)** encender un cigarrillo; **~bulb** el foco
lighter el encendedor
like *v* gustar; **I like** me gusta
line (train) la línea
linen el lino
lip el labio
liquor store la licorería
liter el litro
little chico

live *v* vivir
liver (body part) el hígado
loafers los mocasines
local de la zona
lock *v* cerrar; **~** *n* el cerrojo
locker el casillero
log off *v* **(computer)** cerrar sesión
log on *v* **(computer)** iniciar sesión
long largo; **~-sighted [BE]** hipermétrope; **~ sleeves** las mangas largas;
look *v* mirar
lose *v* **(something)** perder
lost perdido; **~ and found** la oficina de objetos perdidos
lotion la loción
love *v* querer; **~** *n* el amor
low bajo
luggage el equipaje; **~ cart** el carrito de equipaje; **~ locker** el casillero automático; **~ ticket** el talón de equipaje; **hand ~ [BE]** el equipaje de mano
lunch la comida
lung el pulmón

M

magazine la revista
magnificent magnífico
mail *v* enviar por correo; **~** *n* el correo; **~box** el buzón de correo
main principal; **~ attractions** los principales sitios de interés; **~ course** el plato principal
make up a prescription *v* **[BE]** surtir medicamentos
mall el centro comercial
man el hombre
manager el gerente
manicure el manicure
manual car el auto con transmisión manual
map el mapa
market el mercado
married casado
marry *v* casarse
mass (church service) la misa
massage el masaje
match el fósforo
meal la comida
measure *v* **(someone)** medir
measuring cup la taza medidora
measuring spoon la cuchara medidora
mechanic el mecánico
medicine el medicamento
medium (size) mediano
meet *v* **(someone)** conocer
meeting la reunión; **~ room** la sala de reuniones
membership card la tarjeta de membresía
memorial (place) el monumento conmemorativo
memory card la tarjeta de memoria
mend *v* zurcir
menstrual cramps los cólicos menstruales
menu la carta
message el mensaje
meter (parking) el estacionómetro
Mexican mexicano
Mexico México
microwave el microondas
midday [BE] el mediodía
midnight la medianoche

mileage el kilometraje
mini-bar el minibar
minute el minuto
missing perdido
mistake el error
mobile móvil; **~ home** casa rodante; **~ phone [BE]** el teléfono celular
mobility la movilidad
money el dinero
month el mes
mop el trapeador
moped la bicimoto
more más
morning la mañana
mosque la mezquita
mother la madre
motion sickness el mareo
motor el motor; **~ boat** la lancha de motor; **~cycle** la motocicleta; **~way [BE]** la autopista
mountain la montaña; **~ bike** la bicicleta de montaña
mousse (hair) el mousse para el pelo
mouth la boca
movie la película; **~ theater** el cine
mug *v* asaltar
muscle (body part) el músculo
museum el museo
music la música; **~ store** la tienda de música

N

nail la uña; **~ file** la lima de uñas; **~ salon** el salón de manicure
name el nombre
napkin la servilleta
nappy [BE] el pañal
nationality la nacionalidad
nature preserve la reserva natural
(be) nauseous *v* tener náuseas
near cerca; **~by** cerca de aquí; **~-sighted** miope
neck el cuello
necklace el collar
need *v* necesitar
newspaper el periódico
newsstand el puesto de periódicos
next siguiente
nice amable
night la noche; **~club** la discoteca
no no
non sin; **~-alcoholic** sin alcohol; **~-smoking** para no fumadores
noon el mediodía
north el norte
nose la nariz
note [BE] el billete
nothing nada
notify *v* avisar
novice (skill level) principiante
now ahora
number el número
nurse el enfermero♂/la enfermera♀

O

office la oficina; **~ hours (doctor's)** las horas de consulta; **~ hours (other offices)** el horario de oficina
off-licence [BE] licorería
oil el aceite
OK de acuerdo
old viejo

on the corner en la esquina
once una vez
one un, uno; **~-way ticket** el boleto sencillo
only solamente
open *v* abrir; *~adj* abierto
opera la ópera; **~ house** el teatro de la ópera
opposite frente a
optician el oculista
orange (color) naranja
orchestra la orquesta
order *v* pedir
outdoor pool la alberca exterior
outside fuera
over sobre; **~ the counter (medication)** sin receta; **~look (scenic place)** el mirador; **~night** por la noche
oxygen treatment la oxígenoterapia

P

pacifier el chupón
pack *v* hacer las maletas
package el paquete
paddling pool [BE] el chapoteadero
pad [BE] la toalla sanitaria
pain el dolor
pajamas las pijamas
palace el palacio
pants los pantalones
pantyhose las medias
paper el papel; **~ towel** toallas de papel
paracetamol [BE] el paracetamol
park *v* estacionar; **~** *n* el parque; **~ing garage** el garage; **~ing lot** el estacionamiento
parliament building el palacio de justicia
part (for car) la pieza; **~-time** medio tiempo
pass through *v* estar de paso
passenger el pasajero
passport el pasaporte; **~control** migración
password la contraseña
pastry shop la pastelería
path el camino
pay *v* pagar; **~ phone** el teléfono público
peak (of a mountain) la cima
pearl la perla
pedestrian el peatón
pediatrician el pediatra
pedicure el pedicure
pen la pluma
penicillin la penicilina
penis el pene
per por; **~ day** por día; **~ hour** por hora; **~ night** por noche; **~ week** por semana
perfume el perfume
period (menstrual) la regla; **~ (of time)** la época
permit *v* permitir
personal identification number (PIN) el número de identificación personal (NIP)
pesos (Mexican currency) pesos
petite las tallas pequeñas
petrol [BE] la gasolina; **~ station [BE]** la gasolinera
pewter el pewter

pharmacy la farmacia
phone *v* hacer una llamada; ~*n* el teléfono; ~ **call** la llamada de teléfono; ~ **card** la tarjeta de teléfono; ~ **number** el número de teléfono
photo la foto; ~**copy** la fotocopia; ~**graphy** la fotografía
pick up *v* **(something)** recoger
picnic area el área para día de campo
piece el trozo
pill (birth control) el anticonceptivo
pillow la almohada
piste [BE] la pista; ~ **map [BE]** el mapa de pistas
pizzeria la pizzería
place *v* **(a bet)** hacer una apuesta
plane el avión
plastic wrap el plástico transparente
plate el plato
platform [BE] (train) el andén
platinum el platino
play *v* jugar; ~ *n* **(theater)** la obra de teatro; ~**ground** el patio de recreo
please por favor
pleasure el placer
plunger el destapador
plus size la talla extra
pocket el bolsillo
poison el veneno
police la policía; ~ **report** la denuncia; ~ **station** la comisaría
pond el estanque
pool la alberca
pop music la música pop
portion la porción
post [BE] el correo; ~ **office** la oficina de correos; ~**box [BE]** el buzón de correos; ~**card** la postal
pot la olla
pottery la cerámica
pounds (British sterling) las libras esterlinas
pregnant embarazada
prescribe *v* recetar
prescription la receta
press *v* **(clothing)** planchar
price el precio
print *v* imprimir
problem el problema
produce las frutas y verduras; ~ **store** la frutería y verdulería
prohibit *v* prohibir
pronounce *v* pronunciar
public el público
pull *v* **(door sign)** jalar
purse el bolso
push *v* **(door sign)** empujar; ~**chair [BE]** el coche de niño

Q

quality la calidad
question la pregunta
quiet tranquilo

R

racetrack la pista de carreras
racket (sports) la raqueta
railway station [BE] la estación del tren
rain la lluvia; ~**coat** el impermeable; ~**forest** el bosque pluvial; ~**y** lluvioso

rap (music) el rap
rape *v* violar; ~*n* la violación
rash el salpullido
razor blade la hoja de afeitar
reach *v* localizar
ready listo
real auténtico
receipt el recibo
receive *v* recibir
reception la recepción
recharge *v* recargar
recommend *v* recomendar
recommendation la recomendación
recycle *v* reciclar
refrigerator el refrigerador
region la región
registered mail el correo certificado
regular normal
relationship la relación
rent *v* rentar
rental car el auto rentado
repair *v* arreglar
repeat *v* repetir
reservation la reserva; **~ desk** la taquilla
reserve *v* reservar
restaurant el restaurante
restroom el sanitario
retired jubilado
return *v* **(something)** devolver; ~ *n* **[BE](trip)** redondo
rib (body part) la costilla
right (direction) derecha; **~ of way** derecho de paso
ring el anillo
river el río
road map el mapa de carreteras
rob robar
robbed robado
romantic romántico
room la habitación; **~ key** la llave de habitación; **~ service** el servicio al cuarto
round-trip viaje redondo
route la ruta
rowboat el bote de remos
rubbish [BE] la basura; **~ bag [BE]** la bolsa de basura
rugby el rubgy
ruins las ruinas
rush la prisa

S

sad triste
safe *n* la caja fuerte; ~*adj* seguro
sales tax el IVA
same mismo
sandals las sandalias
sanitary napkin la toalla sanitaria
saucepan la cacerola
sauna el sauna
save *v* **(computer)** guardar
savings (account) la cuenta de ahorros
scanner el escáner
scarf la bufanda
schedule *v* programar; ~*n* el horario
school la escuela
scissors las tijeras
sea el mar
seat el asiento
security la seguridad
see *v* ver
self-service el autoservicio
sell *v* vender
seminar el seminario

send *v* enviar
senior citizen anciano
separated (marriage) separado
serious serio
service (in a restaurant) el servicio
sexually transmitted disease (STD) la enfermedad venérea
shampoo el champú
sharp afilado
shaving cream la crema para afeitar
sheet la sábana
ship *v* enviar
shirt la camisa
shoe store la zapatería
shoes los zapatos
shop *v* comprar
shopping ir de compras;
 ~ **area** la zona de compras;
 ~ **centre [BE]** el centro comercial;
 ~ **mall** el centro comercial
short corto; ~ **sleeves** las mangas cortas;
 ~**s** los pantalones cortos;
 ~**-sighted [BE]** miope
shoulder el hombro
show *v* enseñar
shower la regadera
shrine el santuario
sick enfermo
side el lado;
 ~ **dish** la guarnición;
 ~ **effect** el efecto secundario;
 ~ **order** la guarnición
sightsee *v* hacer turismo
sightseeing tour el recorrido turístico
sign *v* **(name)** firmar
silk la seda
silver la plata
single (unmarried) soltero;
 ~ **bed** la cama individual;
 ~ **room** una habitación individual
sink el lavabo
sister la hermana
sit *v* sentarse
size la talla
skin la piel
skirt la falda
sleep *v* dormir; ~**er car** vagón dormitorio; ~**ing bag** el saco de dormir
slice *v* cortar en rodajas
slippers las pantuflas
slow despacio
slowly despacio
small chico
smoke *v* fumar
smoking (area) área de fumadores
snack bar la cafetería
sneakers los tenis
snorkeling equipment el equipo de esnórquel
soap el jabón
soccer el fútbol
sock el calcetín
some alguno
soother [BE] el chupón
sore throat garganta irritada
sorry lo siento
south el sur
souvenir el recuerdo; ~ **store** la tienda de recuerdos
spa spa
Spanish el español

spatula la espátula
speak *v* hablar
special (food) la especialidad de la casa
specialist (doctor) el especialista
specimen el ejemplar
speeding el exceso de velocidad
spell *v* deletrear
spicy picante
spine (body part) la columna vertebral
spoon la cuchara
sports los deportes; ~ **massage** el masaje deportivo
sporting goods store la tienda de artículos deportivos
sprain el esguince
square cuadrado; ~ **kilometer** el kilómetro cuadrado; ~ **meter** el metro cuadrado
stadium el estadio
stairs las escaleras
stamp *v* **(a ticket)** marcar; ~ *n* **(postage)** la estampilla
start *v* empezar
starter [BE] el aperitivo
station la estación; **bus ~** la estación de camiones; **gas ~** la gasolinera; **petrol ~ [BE]** la gasolinera; **railway ~ [BE]** la estación del tren; **underground ~ [BE]** la estación del metro
statue la estatua
stay *v* quedarse
steal *v* robar
steep empinado
sterling silver la plata de ley
sting la picazón
stolen robado
stomach el estómago; **~ache** el dolor de estómago
stop *v* parar; ~ *n* la parada
store directory el directorio de tiendas
storey [BE] la planta
stove el horno
straight de frente
strange extraño
stream el arroyo
stroller la carreola
student el estudiante
study *v* estudiar
studying estudiando
stunning impresionante
subtitle el subtítulo
subway el metro; ~ **station** la estación del metro
suit el traje
suitcase la maleta
sun el sol; **~block** el bloqueador solar; **~burn** la quemadura solar; **~glasses** los lentes oscuros; **~ny** soleado; **~screen** el protector solar; **~stroke** la insolación
supermarket el supermercado
surfboard la tabla de surf
surgical spirit [BE] el alcohol etílico
swallow *v* tragar
sweater el suéter
sweatshirt la sudadera
sweet (taste) dulce;
swelling la hinchazón
swim *v* nadar; **~suit** traje de baño
symbol (keyboard) el símbolo
synagogue la sinagoga

T

table la mesa
tablet (medicine) la pastilla
take *v* llevar; **~ away [BE]** para llevar
tampon el tampón
taste *v* probar
taxi el taxi
team el equipo
teaspoon la cucharadita
telephone el teléfono
temple (religious) el templo
temporary temporal
tennis el tenis
tent la tienda de campaña; **~ peg** la estaca; **~ pole** el palo
terminal (airport) la terminal
terracotta la terracota
terrible terrible
text *v* **(send a message)** enviar un mensaje de texto; **~** *n* **(message)** el texto
thank *v* dar las gracias a; **~ you** gracias
that eso
theater el teatro
theft el robo
there ahí
thief el ladrón
thigh el muslo
thirsty sediento
this esto
throat la garganta
ticket el boleto; **~ office** la taquilla
tie (clothing) la corbata
time el tiempo; **~table [BE]** el horario
tire la rueda
tired cansado
tissue el pañuelo de papel
tobacconist la tabaquería
today hoy
toe el dedo del pie; **~nail** la uña del pie
toilet [BE] el sanitario; **~ paper** el papel higiénico
tomorrow mañana
tongue la lengua
tonight esta noche
too demasiado
tooth el diente; **~brush** el cepillo de dientes; **~paste** la pasta de dientes
total (amount) el total
tough (food) duro
tourist el turista; **~ information office** la oficina de turismo
tour el recorrido turístico
tow truck la grúa
towel la toalla
tower la torre
town la ciudad; **~ hall** el ayuntamiento; **~ map** el mapa de ciudad; **~ square** la plaza
toy el juguete; **~ store** la juguetería
track (train) el andén
traditional tradicional
traffic light el semáforo
trail la pista; **~ map** el mapa de la pista
trailer el remolque
train el tren; **~ station** la estación del tren
transfer *v* cambiar

translate *v* traducir
trash la basura
travel *v* viajar; **~ agency** la agencia de viajes; **~ sickness** el mareo; **~er's check [cheque BE]** el cheque de viajero
tree el árbol
trim (hair cut) *v* cortarse las puntas
trip el viaje
trolley [BE] el carrito
trousers [BE] los pantalones
T-shirt la camiseta
turn off *v* apagar
turn on *v* encender
TV la televisión
type *v* escribir a máquina
tyre [BE] la rueda

U

ugly feo
umbrella el paraguas
unattended desatendido
unbranded medication [BE] el medicamento genérico
unconscious inconsciente
underground [BE] el metro; **~ station [BE]** la estación del metro
underpants [BE] los calzones
understand *v* entender
underwear la ropa interior
United Kingdom (U.K.) el Reino Unido
United States (U.S.) los Estados Unidos
university la universidad
unleaded (gas) la gasolina sin plomo
upper superior
urgent urgente
use *v* usar
username el nombre de usuario
utensil el cubierto

V

vacancy la habitación libre
vacation las vacaciones
vaccination la vacuna
vacuum cleaner la aspiradora
vagina la vagina
vaginal infection la infección vaginal
validity validez
valley el valle
valuable de valor
value el valor
VAT [BE] el IVA
vegetarian vegetariano
vehicle registration los papeles del auto
viewpoint [BE] el mirador
village el pueblo
vineyard el viñedo
visa (passport document) la visa
visit *v* visitar; **~ing hours** el horario de visita
visually impaired la persona con discapacidad visual
vitamin la vitamina
V-neck el cuello en V
volleyball game el partido de voleibol

vomit *v* vomitar

W

wait *v* esperar; **~** *n* la espera; **~ing room** la sala de espera
waiter el mesero
waitress la mesera
wake *v* despertarse; **~-up call** la llamada despertador
walk *v* caminar; **~** *n* la caminata; **~ing route** la ruta de excursionismo
wall clock el reloj de pared
wallet la cartera
warm *v* calentar; **~** *adj* **(temperature)** calor
washing machine la lavadora
watch el reloj
water skis los esquís acuáticos
waterfall la cascada
weather el tiempo
week la semana; **~end** el fin de semana; **~ly** semanal
welcome *v* acoger; **~** bienvenido
well bien; **~-rested** descansado
west el oeste
what (question) qué
wheelchair la silla de ruedas; **~ ramp** la rampa para la silla de ruedas
when (question) cuándo
where (question) dónde
white gold el oro blanco
who (question) quién
widowed viudo
wife la esposa
window la ventana; **~ case** el aparador
windsurfer el surfista
wine list la carta de vinos
wireless inalámbrico; **~ internet** el acceso de Internet inalámbrico; **~ internet service** el servicio inalámbrico a Internet; **~ phone** el teléfono inalámbrico
with con
withdraw *v* retirar
without sin
woman la mujer
wool la lana
work *v* trabajar
wrap *v* envolver
wrist la muñeca
write *v* escribir

Y

year el año
yellow gold el oro amarillo
yes sí
yesterday ayer
young joven
youth hostel el hostal juvenil

Z

zoo el zoológico

Spanish–English Dictionary

A

la abadía abbey
el abanico fan (souvenir)
abierto *adj* open
el abogado lawyer
abrazar *v* hug
el abrelatas can opener
el abrigo coat
abrir *v* open
los abuelos grandparents
aburrido boring
acampar *v* camp
el acantilado cliff
el acceso access; **~ inalámbrico a Internet** wireless internet; **~ para discapacitados** handicapped-[disabled- BE] accessible
el accidente accident
el aceite oil
aceptar *v* accept
acoger *v* welcome
acompañar a *v* join
el acondicionador conditioner
la acupuntura acupuncture
el adaptador adapter
adicional extra
adiós goodbye
las aduanas customs
el aeropuerto airport
afilado sharp
la agencia agency; **~ de viajes** travel agency
agotado exhausted
el agua water; **~ caliente** hot water; **~ potable** drinking water
el agua de colonia cologne
las aguas termales hot spring
ahí there
ahora now
el aire air; **~ acondicionado** air conditioning
la alberca pool; **~ cubierta** indoor pool; **~ exterior** outdoor pool
algo anything
el algodón cotton
alguno some
alimentar *v* feed
el allanamiento de morada break-in (burglary)
la almohada pillow
el alojamiento accommodation
alto high
amable nice
la ambulancia ambulance
el amigo friend
el amor *n* love
el andén track [platform BE] (train)
anémico anemic
la anestesia anesthesia
el anillo ring
el animal animal
antes de before
el antibiótico antibiotic
el antro bar, club
el año year
apagar *v* turn off
el aparador window case
el apéndice appendix (body part)
el aperitivo appetizer [starter BE]
aquí here
el árbol tree
la aromaterapia aromatherapy
arreglar *v* repair
el arroyo stream

la arteria artery
la articulación joint (body part)
los artículos goods; **~ para el hogar** household good
la artritis arthritis
asaltar *v* mug
el asalto attack
el asiento seat; **~ de pasillo** aisle seat; **~ para niños** car seat;
asistir *v* attend
asmático asthmatic
la aspiradora vacuum cleaner
la aspirina aspirin
los audífonos headphones
Australia Australia
australiano Australian
auténtico real
el auto car; **~ automático** automatic car; **~ cama** sleeper [sleeping BE] car; **~ con transmisión manual** manual car; **~ rentado** rental [hire BE] car
automático automatic
la autopista highway [motorway BE]
el autoservicio self-service
la avería breakdown
el avión airplane, plane
avisar *v* notify
ayer yesterday
la ayuda *n* help
ayudar *v* help
el ayuntamiento town hall
azul blue

B

bailar *v* dance
bajarse *v* get off (a train, bus, subway)
bajo low
el ballet ballet
el banco bank
el baño bathroom
barato cheap, inexpensive
el barco boat
el básquetbol basketball
la basura trash [rubbish BE]
la batería battery (car)
el bebé baby
beber *v* drink
la bebida *n* drink
beige beige
el béisbol baseball
las bellas artes arts
besar *v* kiss
el biberón baby bottle
la biblioteca library
la bicicleta bicycle; **~ de montaña** mountain bike
bienvenido welcome
el billete *n* bill (money)
el bikini bikini
blanco white
el bloqueador solar sunscreen
la blusa blouse
la boca mouth
el boleto ticket; **~ de ida** one-way ticket; **~ del camión** bus ticket; **~ electrónico** e-ticket; **~ redondo** round trip [return BE] ticket
la bolsa de basura garbage [rubbish BE] bag
el bolsillo pocket
el bolso purse [handbag BE]
los bomberos fire department
bonito cute
borrar *v* clear (on an ATM); **~** *v* delete (computer)

el bosque forest; **~ pluvial** rainforest
las botas boots;
~ de montaña hiking boots
el bote jar
el bote de remos rowboat
la botella bottle
el brazo arm
británico British
el broche brooch
bucear to dive
buenas noches good evening
buenas tardes good afternoon
bueno *adj* good
buenos días good morning
la bufanda scarf
el buzón de correo mailbox [postbox BE]

C

la cabaña cabin (house)
la cabeza head (body part)
la cacerola saucepan
el café Internet internet cafe
la cafetería cafe, coffee shop, snack bar
la caja box; **~ de cigarros** carton of cigarettes
la caja fuerte *n* safe
el cajero cashier;
~ automático ATM
el calcetín sock
la calefacción heater [heating BE]
calentar *v* heat, warm
la calidad quality
calor hot, warm (temperature)
las calorías calories
los calzones briefs [underpants BE] (clothing)
la cama single bed;
~ matrimonial double bed
la cámara camera;
~ digital digital camera
el camarote cabin (ship)
el camastro deck chair
cambiar *v* change, exchange, transfer
el cambio *n* change (money);
~ de divisas currency exchange
caminar *v* walk
la caminata *n* walk
el camino path
el camión bus; **~ rápido** express bus
la camisa shirt
la camiseta T-shirt
el campamento campsite
el campo field (sports);
~ de batalla battleground;
~ de golf golf course
Canadá Canada
canadiense Canadian
cancelar *v* cancel
el candado *n* lock
cansado tired
el cañón canyon
la cara face
el carbón charcoal
el carnicero butcher
caro expensive
el carrito cart [trolley BE] (grocery store); **~ de equipaje** luggage cart
la carta letter
la carta menu;
~ de bebidas drink menu;
~ de vinos wine list;
~ para niños children's menu
la cartera wallet
la casa house; **~ de cambio** currency exchange office

la casa rodante mobile home
casado married
casarse *v* marry
la cascada waterfall
el casco helmet
el casillero luggage locker
el castillo castle
el catarro cold (sickness)
la catedral cathedral
el catre cot
causar daño *v* damage
el CD CD
la cena dinner
el centímetro centimeter
el centro downtown area; **~ comercial** shopping mall [centre BE]; **~ de negocios** business center
el cepillo de pelo hair brush
la cerámica pottery
cerca near; **~ de aquí** nearby
el cerillo *n* match
cerrado closed
cerrar *v* close, lock; **~ sesión** *v* log off (computer)
el certificado certificate
la cesta basket (grocery store)
el chaleco salvavidas life jacket
el champú shampoo
chapoteadero kiddie [paddling BE] pool
la chaqueta jacket
el cheque *n* check [cheque BE] (payment); **~ de viajero** traveler's check [cheque BE]
el chicle chewing gum
chico small
chocar *v* crash (car)
el chupón pacifier [soother BE]
el ciclismo cycling
la ciencia science
el cigarrillo cigarette
la cima peak (of a mountain)
el cine movie theater
la cinta transportadora conveyor belt
el cinturón belt
la cita appointment
la ciudad town
la clase class; **~ ejecutiva** business class; **~ turista** economy class
el club de jazz jazz club
la cobija blanket
cobrar *v* bill (charge); **~** *v* cash; **~** *v* charge (credit card)
el cobre copper
la carriola stroller [pushchair BE]
la cocina kitchen
cocinar *v* cook
el código area code
el código de país country code
el codo elbow
el colador colander
los cólicos menstruales menstrual cramps
la colina hill
el collar necklace
el color color
la columna vertebral spine (body part)
el comedor dining room
comer *v* eat
la comida food, lunch, meal; **~ rápida** fast food
cómo how
el compañero de trabajo colleague
la compañía company; **~ aérea** airline; **~ de seguros** insurance company
comprar *v* buy, shop
la computadora computer
con with

el concierto concert
el condón condom
conducir *v* drive
conectarse *v* connect (internet)
la conexión connection (internet); **~ de vuelo** connection (flight)
la conferencia conference
confirmar *v* confirm
el congelador freezer
la congestión congestion
conocer *v* meet (someone)
el consulado Consulate
el consultor consultant
contagioso contagious
la contraseña password
el corazón heart
la corbata tie (clothing)
el correo *n* mail [post BE]; **~ aéreo** airmail; **~ certificado** registered mail; **~ electrónico** *n* e-mail
cortar *v* cut (hair); **~ en rodajas** to slice
cortarse las puntas *v* trim (hair cut)
el corte *n* cut (injury); **~ de pelo** haircut
corto short
costar *v* cost
la costilla rib (body part)
la crema cream; **~ antiséptica** antiseptic cream; **~ de afeitar** shaving cream; **~hidratante** lotion
el cristal crystal
el cruce intersection
la cruda hangover
cuándo when (question)
cuánto cuesta how much
el cubierto utensil
la cuchara spoon; **~ medidora** measuring spoon
la cucharadita teaspoon
la cuchilla desechable disposable razor
el cuchillo knife
el cuello neck; **~ en V** V-neck; **~ redondo** crew neck
la cuenta account; **~ corriente** checking [current BE] account; **~ de ahorros** savings account
cuero leather
la cueva cave
el cumpleaños birthday
la cuna crib
la curita bandage

D

dar to give; **~ fuego** light (cigarette); **~ las gracias a** *v* thank; **~ pecho** breastfeed
de from, of; **~ acuerdo** OK; **~ la mañana** a.m.; **~ la tarde** p.m.; **~ la zona** local
declarar *v* declare
el dedo finger; **~ del pie** toe
de frente straight
deletrear *v* spell
delicioso delicious
la dentadura denture
el dentista dentist
dentro in
el departamento apartment
la depilacion wax; **~ de cejas** eyebrow wax; **~ de las ingles** bikini wax
deportes sports
depositar *v* deposit
el depósito bancario deposit (bank)
la derecha right (direction)
el derecho de paso right of way

desaparecido missing
desatendido unattended
el desayuno breakfast
descansado well-rested
desconectar *v* disconnect (computer)
el descuento discount
desechable disposable
el desierto desert
el desodorante deodorant
despacio slowly
despertarse *v* wake
después after
el destapador bottle opener
el destapador plunger
el detergente detergent
detrás de behind (direction)
devolver *v* exchange, return (goods)
el día day
diabético diabetic
el diamante diamond
la diarrea diarrhea
el diente tooth
el diésel diesel
difícil difficult
digital digital
el dinero money
la dirección address; **~ de correo electrónico** e-mail address
discapacitado handicapped [disabled BE]
la discoteca club (dance, night); **~ gay** gay club
disculparse *v* excuse (to get attention)
disfrutar *v* enjoy
disponible available
divorciar *v* divorce
doblado dubbed
doblando (la esquina) around (the corner)
la docena dozen
el doctor doctor
la documentación check-in (airport)
documentar check (luggage)
el dólar dollar (U.S.)
el dolor pain; **~ de cabeza** headache; **~ de espalda** backache; **~ de estómago** stomachache; **~ de oído** earache; **~ de pecho** chest pain
dónde where (question)
dormir *v* sleep
el dormitorio dormitory
dulce sweet (taste)
durante during
el DVD DVD

E

la edad age
el edificio building
el efectivo cash
el efecto secundario side effect
el ejemplar specimen
el elevador elevator [lift BE]
embarazada pregnant
embarcar *v* board
empezar *v* begin, start
empinado steep
empujar *v* push (door sign)
en la esquina on the corner
el encaje lace
el encendedor lighter
encender *v* turn on
el enchufe electric outlet
la enfermedad venérea sexually

transmitted disease (STD)
el enfermero♂**/la enfermera**♀ nurse
enfermo sick
enseñar *v* show
entender *v* understand
la entrada admission/cover charge; ~ entrance
entrar *v* enter
el entretenimiento entertainment
enviar *v* send, ship; **~ por correo** *v* mail; **~ un correo electrónico** *v* e-mail; **~ un fax** *v* fax ; **~ un mensaje de texto** *v* text (send a message)
envolver *v* wrap
la época period (of time)
el equipaje luggage [baggage BE]; **~ de mano** carry-on (piece of hand luggage)
el equipo team; equipment; **~ de buceo** diving equipment; **~ de esnórquel** snorkeling equipment
el error mistake
las escaleras stairs; **~ eléctricas** escalators
el escáner scanner
la escoba broom
escribir *v* write; **~ a máquina** *v* type
la escuela school
el esguince sprain
el esmalte enamel (jewelry)
eso that
la espalda back
el español Spanish
la espátula spatula
la especialidad de la casa special (food)
el especialista specialist (doctor)
la espera *n* wait
esperar *v* wait
los esquís acuáticos water skis
esta noche tonight
la estaca tent peg
la estación station; **~ de camiones** bus station; **~ del metro** subway [underground BE] station; **~ de policía** police station **~ del tren** train [railway BE] station
el estacionamiento parking garage; ~ parking lot [car park BE]
estacionar *v* park
el estadio stadium
el estado de salud condition (medical)
los Estados Unidos United States (U.S.)
estadounidense American
la estampilla *n* stamp (postage)
el estanque pond
estar *v* be
la estatua statue
el este east
el estilista hairstylist
esto this
el estómago stomach
estreñido constipated
el estuche para la cámara camera case
estudiando studying
estudiar *v* study
la estufa stove
la estufa portátil camp stove
el euro euro
el exceso excess; **~ de velocidad** speeding

la excursión excursion
el excusado químico chemical toilet
experto expert (skill level)
la extensión extension (phone)
extra grande extra large
extraer *v* extract (tooth)
extraño strange

F

el facial facial
fácil easy
la factura bill [invoice BE]
la falda skirt
la familia family
la farmacia pharmacy [chemist BE]
el fax *n* fax
la fecha date (calendar)
feliz happy
feo ugly
la fianza deposit (to reserve a room)
la fiebre fever
el fin de semana weekend
firmar *v* sign (name)
la flor flower
el foco lightbulb
la fórmula formula (baby)
el formulario form
la foto exposure (film); ~ photo; **~ digital** digital photo; **~copia** photocopy; **~grafía** photography
los frenos brakes (car)
frente a opposite
fresco fresh
frío cold (temperature)
las frutas y verduras produce
la frutería y verdulería produce store
el fuego fire
la fuente fountain
fuera outside
el fuerte fort
fumar *v* smoke
el fútbol soccer [football BE]

G

el garaje garage (parking)
la garganta throat
la garganta irritada sore throat
el gas butano cooking gas
la gasolina gas [petrol BE]; **~ sin plomo** unleaded gas
la gasolinera gas [petrol BE] station
gay gay
el gel gel (hair)
el gerente manager
el gimnasio gym
el ginecólogo gynecologist
la gota drop (medicine)
grabar *v* burn (CD); ~ *v* engrave
gracias thank you
los grados degrees (temperature); **~ centígrado** Celsius
el gramo gram
grande large
la granja farm
gratuito free
gris gray
la grúa tow truck
el grupo group
guapo attractive
guardar *v* save (computer)
la guarnición side dish, order
el guía guide
la guía guide book; **~ de tiendas**

store directory
gustar *v* like; **me gusta** I like

H

la habitación room; **~ libre** vacancy; **~ sencilla** single room
hablar *v* speak
hacer *v* do; **~ una apuesta** *v* place (a bet); **~ un arreglo** *v* alter; **~ una llamada** *v* phone; **~ las maletas** *v* pack; **~ turismo** sightseeing
hambriento hungry
helado *adj* frozen
la hermana sister
el hermano brother
el hielo ice
el hígado liver (body part)
la hinchazón swelling
hipermétrope far-sighted [long-sighted BE]
el hipódromo horsetrack
el hockey hockey; **~ sobre hielo** ice hockey
la hoja de afeitar razor blade
hola hello
el hombre man
el hombro shoulder
hondo deep
la hora hour
el horario *n* schedule [timetable BE]
los horarios hours; **~ de atención al público** business hours; **~ de oficina** office hours; **~ de visita** visiting hours
las horas de consulta office hours (doctor's)
el horno oven
el hospital hospital
el hostal hostel; **~ juvenil** youth hostel
el hotel hotel
hoy today
el hueso bone

I

el ibuprofeno ibuprofen
la identificación identification
la iglesia church
el impermeable raincoat
impresionante stunning
imprimir *v* print
el impuesto duty (tax)
incluir *v* include
inconsciente unconscious
increíble amazing
la infección vaginal vaginal infection
infectado infected
el inglés English
iniciar sesión *v* log on (computer)
el insecto bug
insípido bland
la insolación sunstroke
el insomnio insomnia
la insulina insulin
interesante interesting
internacional international (airport area)
el Internet internet
el intérprete interpreter
el intestino intestine
intolerante intolerant; **~ a la lactosa** lactose intolerant
introducir *v* insert
ir a *v* go (somewhere)
ir de compras *v* go shopping

Irlanda Ireland
irlandés Irish
el IVA sales tax [VAT BE]
la izquierda left (direction)

J

el jabón soap
jalar *v* pull (door sign)
el jardín botánico botanical garden
la jarra carafe
el jazz jazz
los jeans jeans
joven young
las joyas jewelry
la joyería jeweler's
jubilado retired
jugar *v* play
el juguete toy

K

el kilo kilo; **~gramo** kilogram; **~metraje** mileage
el kilómetro kilometer; **~ cuadrado** square kilometer

L

el labio lip
la laca hairspray
el ladrón thief
el lago lake
la lana wool
la lancha motora motor boat
largo long
el lavabo sink
la lavadora washing machine
la lavandería laundromat [launderette BE]
lavar *v* wash
lavar la ropa laundry
el lavaplatos dishwasher
la lección lesson
lejos far
la lengua tongue
la lente lens
los lentes glasses; **~ de contacto** contact lenses; **~ oscuros** sunglasses
las libras esterlinas pounds (British sterling)
libre de impuestos duty-free
la librería bookstore
el libro book
la lima de uñas nail file
limpiar *v* clean
limpio *adj* clean
la línea line (train)
el lino linen
la linterna flashlight
el líquido liquid; **~ de lentes de contacto** contact lens solution; **~ lavaplatos** dishwashing liquid
listo ready
la litera berth
el litro liter
la llamada *n* call; **~ de teléfono** phone call; **~ despertador** wake-up call
llamar *v* call
la llanta tire [tyre BE]; **~ ponchada** flat tire [tyre BE]
la llave key; **~ de habitación** room key; **~ electrónica** key card
el llavero key ring
las llegadas arrivals (airport)
llegar *v* arrive
llenar *v* fill
llevar *v* take; **~ en auto** lift (to give a ride)

la lluvia rain
lluvioso rainy
lo siento sorry
localizar *v* reach
la loción para después de afeitar aftershave
la luz light (overhead)

M

la madre mother
magnífico magnificent
el malestar estomacal upset stomach
la maleta bag, suitcase
la mandíbula jaw
las mangas cortas short sleeves
las mangas largas long sleeves
el manicure manicure
la mano hand
mañana tomorrow; **la ~** morning
el mapa map; **~ de carreteras** road map; **~ de ciudad** town map; **~ de la pista** trail [piste BE] map
el mar sea
marcar *v* dial
mareado dizzy
el mareo motion [travel BE] sickness
el marido husband
el martillo hammer
más more
el masaje massage; **~ deportivo** sports massage
el mecánico mechanic
la media hora half hour
mediano medium (size)
la medianoche midnight
el medicamento medicine
medio half; **~ kilo** half-kilo; **~día** noon [midday BE]
medir *v* measure (someone)
mejor best
menos less
el mensaje message; **~ instantáneo** instant message
el mercado market
el mes month
la mesa table
la mesera waitress
el mesero waiter
el mesón bed and breakfast
el metro subway [underground BE]
el metro cuadrado square meter
México Mexico
mexicano Mexican
la mezclilla denim
la mezquita mosque
el microondas microwave
migración passport control
el minibar mini-bar
el minuto minute
el mirador overlook [viewpoint BE] (scenic place)
mirar *v* look
la misa mass (church service)
mismo same
los mocasines loafers
la mochila backpack
el módulo de información information desk
molestar *v* bother
la moneda coin, currency
la montaña mountain
el monumento conmemorativo memorial (place)
mostrar *v* display
la moto acuática jet ski
la motocicleta motorcycle

la motoneta moped
el mousse para el pelo mousse (hair)
movilidad mobility
la mujer wife, woman
la multa fine (fee for breaking law)
la muñeca doll; ~ wrist
el músculo muscle
el museo museum
la música music; ~ **clásica** classical music; ~ **folclórica** folk music; ~ **pop** pop music
el muslo thigh

N

nacional domestic
la nacionalidad nationality
nada nothing
nadar *v* swim
las nalgas buttocks
naranja orange (color, fruit)
la nariz nose
necesitar *v* need
los negocios business
nevado snowy
el nieto grandchild
la niña girl
la niñera babysitter
el niño boy, child
el nivel intermedio intermediate
no no
la noche evening, night
el nombre name; ~ **de usuario** username
normal regular
las normas de vestimenta dress code
el norte north
la novia girlfriend
el novio boyfriend
el número number; ~ **de fax** fax number; ~ **de identificación personal (NIP)** personal identification number (PIN); ~ **de licencia de conducir** driver's license number; ~ **de teléfono** phone number; ~ **de teléfono de información** information (phone)

O

la obra de teatro *n* play (theater)
el oculista optician
el oeste west
la oficina office; ~ **de correos** post office; ~ **de objetos perdidos** lost and found; ~ **de turismo** tourist information office
el ojo eye
la olla pot
la ópera opera
la oreja ear
la orina urine
el oro gold; ~ **amarillo** yellow gold; ~ **blanco** white gold
la orquesta orchestra
oscuro dark
el otro camino alternate route
la oxígenoterapia oxygen treatment

P

padecer del corazón heart condition
el padre father
pagar *v* pay
el pájaro bird
el palacio palace; ~ **de justicia** parliament building

los palitos chinos chopsticks
el palo tent pole
la panadería bakery
los pantalones pants [trousers BE]; **~ cortos** shorts
las pantuflas slippers
el pañal diaper [nappy BE]
el pañuelo de papel tissue
el papel paper; **~ de aluminio** aluminum [kitchen BE] foil; **~ higiénico** toilet paper
el paquete package
para for; **~ llevar** to go [take away BE]; **~ no fumadores** non-smoking
el paracetamol acetaminophen [paracetamol BE]
la parada *n* stop; **~ del camión** bus stop
el paraguas umbrella
pararse *v* stop
el parque park; **~ de diversiones** amusement park
la parrillada barbecue
el partido game; **~ de fútbol** soccer [football BE]; **~ de voleibol** volleyball game
el pasajero passenger; **~ con boleto** ticketed passenger
el pasaporte passport
el pasillo aisle
la pasta de dientes toothpaste
la pastelería pastry shop
la pastilla tablet (medicine)
el patio de recreo playground
el peatón pedestrian
el pecho chest (body part)
el pediatra pediatrician
el pedicure pedicure
pedir *v* order
el peinado hairstyle
el peine comb
la película movie
peligroso dangerous
el pelo hair
la peluquería barber
los pendientes earrings
el pene penis
la penicilina penicillin
perder *v* lose (something)
perdido lost
el perfume perfume
el periódico newspaper
la periquera highchair
la perla pearl
permitir *v* allow, permit
el perro guía guide dog
la persona con discapacidad visual visually impaired person
pesos pesos (Mexican currency)
el pewter pewter
la picadura de insecto insect bite
picante spicy
picar *v* stamp (a ticket)
la picazón sting
el pie foot
la piel skin
la pierna leg
la pieza part (for car)
la pijama pajamas
la pila battery
la píldora pill (birth control)
la pista trail [piste BE]
la pista de carreras racetrack
la pizzería pizzeria
el placer pleasure
la plancha *n* iron (clothes)
planchar *v* iron
la planta floor [storey BE]; **~ baja** ground floor
el plástico transparente plastic

wrap [cling film BE]
la plata silver; **~ de ley** sterling silver
el platino platinum
el plato dish (kitchen); **~ principal** main course
la playa beach
la plaza town square
la pluma pen
la policía police
la pomada cream (ointment)
ponerse en contacto con *v* contact
por for; **~** per; **~ día** per day; **~ favor** please; **~ hora** per hour; **~ la noche** overnight; **~ noche** per night; **~ semana** per week
la porción portion; **~ para niños** children's portion
el postre dessert
el precio price
precioso beautiful
la pregunta question
presentar *v* introduce
la presión arterial blood pressure
la primera clase first class
primero first
los principales sitios de interés main attraction
principiante beginner, novice (skill level)
la prisa rush
el probador fitting room
probar *v* taste
el problema problem
el producto good; **~ de limpieza** cleaning product
programar *v* schedule
prohibir *v* prohibit
el pronóstico forecast
pronunciar *v* pronounce
provisional temporary
próximo next
el público public
el pueblo village
el puente bridge
la puerta gate (airport); **~** door; **~ de incendios** fire door
el pulmón lung
la pulsera bracelet
el puro cigar

Q

qué what (question)
quedar bien *v* fit (clothing)
quedarse *v* stay
la queja complaint
la quemadura solar sunburn
querer *v* love (someone)
quién who (question)
el quiosco newsstand

R

la rampa para silla de ruedas wheelchair ramp
el rap rap (music)
rápido express, fast
la raqueta racket (sports)
la reacción alérgica allergic reaction
recargar *v* recharge
la recepción reception
la receta prescription
recetar *v* prescribe
rechazar *v* decline (credit card)
recibir *v* receive
el recibo receipt
reciclar recycle
el reclamo de equipaje baggage

claim
recoger *v* pick up (something)
la recomendación recommendation
recomendar *v* recommend
el recorrido tour; **~ en camión** bus tour; **~ turístico** sightseeing tour
el recuerdo souvenir
el refrigerador refrigerator
la regadera shower
el regalo gift
la región region
el registro check-in (hotel); **~ del coche** vehicle registration
la regla period (menstrual)
el Reino Unido United Kingdom (U.K.)
la relación relationship
rellenar *v* fill out (form)
el reloj watch
el remolque trailer
la renta de autos car rental [hire BE]
rentar *v* rent [hire BE]
reparar *v* fix (repair)
el repelente de insectos insect repellent
repetir *v* repeat
la reserva reservation; **~ natural** nature preserve
reservar *v* reserve
respirar *v* breathe
el restaurante restaurant
retirar *v* withdraw
retrasar *v* delay
la reunión meeting
revelar *v* develop (film)
revisar *v* check (on something)
la revista magazine
el riñón kidney (body part)
el río river
robado robbed
robado stolen
robar *v* rob
robar *v* steal
el robo theft
la rodilla knee
rojo red
el rollo film (camera)
romántico romantic
romper *v* break
la ropa clothing; **~ interior** underwear
rosa pink
roto broken
el rubgy rugby
las ruinas ruins
la ruta route; **~ de excursionismo** walking route

S

la sábana sheet
el sacacorchos corkscrew
el saco de dormir sleeping bag
la sala room; **~ de conciertos** concert hall; **~ de espera** waiting room; **~ de reuniones** meeting room
la salchichonería delicatessen
la salida check-out (hotel)
la salida *n* exit; **~ de urgencia** emergency exit
las salidas departures (airport)
salir *v* exit, leave
el salón room; **~ de belleza** hair salon; **~ de convenciones** convention hall; **~ de juegos de video** arcade; **~ de manicure** nail salon
¡Salud! Cheers!
la salud health
el salpullido rash

el salvavidas lifeguard
las sandalias sandals
sangrar *v* bleed
la sangre blood
el santuario shrine
el sartén frying pan
la sauna sauna
el secador de pelo hair dryer
la seda silk
sediento thirsty
la seguridad security
el seguro insurance
seguro safe (protected)
el semáforo traffic light
la semana week
semanal weekly
el seminario seminar
el sendero trail; ~ **para bicicletas** bike route
el seno breast
sentarse *v* sit
sentirse mal *v* be ill
separado separated (marriage)
ser *v* be
serio serious
el servicio restroom [toilet BE]; ~ service (in a restaurant); ~ **completo** full-service; ~ **de habitaciones** room service; ~ **inalámbrico a Internet** wireless internet service; ~ **de Internet** internet service; ~ **de lavandería** laundry service; ~ **de limpieza de habitaciones** housekeeping service
la servilleta napkin
sí yes
el SIDA AIDS
la silla chair; ~ **de ruedas** wheelchair; ~ **para niños** child seat
el símbolo symbol (keyboard)
sin without; ~ **alcohol** non-alcoholic; ~ **receta** over the counter (medication)
la sinagoga synagogue
el sitio de interés attraction (place)
el sobre envelope
el sol sun
solamente only
soleado sunny
solo alone
soltero single (marriage)
el sombrero hat
la somnolencia drowsiness
sordo deaf
el sostén bra
el spa spa
el subtítulo subtitle
sucio dirty
la sudadera sweatshirt
el suelo floor
el suéter sweater
súper super (fuel)
superior upper
el supermercado grocery store, supermarket
la supervisión supervision
el sur south
el surfista windsurfer
surtir la receta *v* fill [make up BE] a prescription

T

la tabaquería tobacconist
la tabla board; ~ **de surf** surfboard
la talla size; ~ **grande** plus size;

~ pequeña petite size
el taller garage (repair)
el talón de equipaje luggage [baggage BE] ticket
el tampón tampon
la tapadura filling (tooth)
la taquilla ticket office
tarde late (time)
la tarde afternoon
la tarifa fee
la tarjeta card; **~ de abordar** boarding pass; **~ de cajero automático** ATM card; **~ de crédito** credit card; **~ de débito** debit card; **~ internacional de estudiante** international student card; **~ de memoria** memory card; **~ postal** postcard; **~ de representación** business card; **~ de seguro** insurance card; **~ de socio** membership card; **~ telefónica** phone card
el taxi taxi
la taza cup; **~ medidora** measuring cup
el tazón bowl
el teatro theater; **~ de la ópera** opera house
la tela impermeable groundcloth [groundsheet BE]
el teleférico cable car
el teléfono telephone; **~ móvil** cell [mobile BE] phone; **~ público** pay phone
la televisión TV
el templo temple (religious)
temprano early
el tenedor fork
tener *v* have; **~ dolor** *v* hurt (have pain); **~ náuseas** *v* be nauseous
el tenis tennis
los tenis sneakers
la terminal terminal (airport)
terminar *v* end
la terracota terracotta
terrible terrible
el texto *n* text (message)
el tiempo time; **~** weather
la tienda store; **~ de alimentos naturales** health food store; **~ de antigüedades** antique store; **~ de bebidas alcohólicas** liquor store [off-licence BE]; **~ de campaña** tent; **~ de deportes** sporting goods store; **~ de fotografía** camera store; **~ de juguetes** toy store; **~ de música** music store; **~ de recuerdos** souvenir store; **~ de regalos** gift shop; **~ de ropa** clothing store
las tiendas departamentales department store
las tijeras scissors
la tintorería dry cleaner
el tipo de cambio exchange rate
la toalla towel; **~ de papel** paper towel; **~ sanitaria** sanitary napkin [pad BE]
la toallita baby wipe
el tobillo ankle
el torneo de golf golf tournament
la torre tower
la tos *n* cough
toser *v* cough
el total total (amount)
trabajar *v* work
tradicional traditional
traducir *v* translate
traer *v* bring